The Kiss and Other Stories

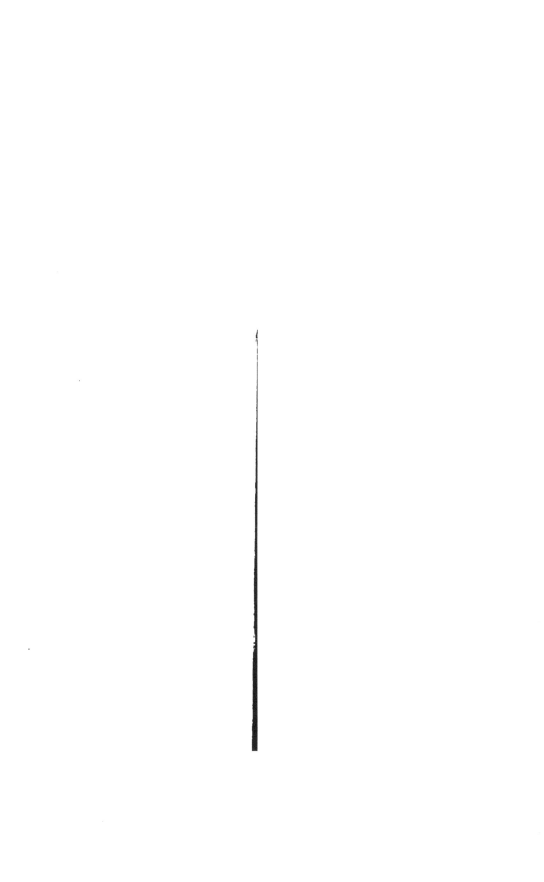

THE KISS
AND OTHER STORIES

"THE KISS,,
"AND OTHER STORIES

By

Anton Tchekhoff

Translated from the Russian by

R. E. C. Long

NEW YORK
FREDERICK A. STOKES COMPANY
1915

614
46

Printed in Great Britain by William Brendon & Son, Ltd., Plymouth

F

CONTENTS

THE KISS

THE KISS

O N the evening of the twentieth of May, at eight
o'clock, all six batteries of the N Artillery
Brigade on their way to camp arrived at the village
of Miestetchki with the intention of spending the
night.

The confusion was at its worst—some officers
fussed about the guns, others in the church square
arranged with the quartermaster—when from behind
the church rode a civilian upon a most remarkable
mount. The small, short-tailed bay with well-shaped
neck progressed with a wobbly motion, all the time
making dance-like movements with its legs as if
some one were switching its hoofs. When he had
drawn rein level with the officers the rider doffed his
cap and said ceremoniously—

"His Excellency, General von Rabbek, whose house
is close by, requests the honour of the officers' company
at tea. . . ."

The horse shook its head, danced, and wobbled to
the rear; its rider again took off his cap, and, turning
his strange steed, disappeared behind the church.

" The devil take it ! " was the general exclamation as the officers dispersed to their quarters. " We can hardly keep our eyes open, yet along comes this von Rabbek with his tea ! I know that tea ! "

The officers of the six batteries had lively memories of a past invitation.   During recent manœuvres they had been asked, together with their Cossack comrades, to tea at the house of a local country gentleman, an officer in retirement, by title a Count ; and this hearty, hospitable Count overwhelmed them with attentions, fed them to satiety, poured vodka down their throats, and made them stay the night.   All this, of course, they enjoyed.   The trouble was that the old soldier entertained his guests too well.   He kept them up till daybreak while he poured forth tales of past adventures ; he dragged them from room to room to point out valuable paintings, old engravings, and rare arms ; he read them holograph letters from celebrated men. And the weary officers, bored to death, listened, gaped, yearned for their beds, and yawned cautiously in their sleeves, until at last when their host released them it was too late for sleep.

Was von Rabbek another old Count ? It might easily be.   But there was no neglecting his invitation. The officers washed and dressed, and set out for von Rabbek's house.   At the church square they learnt that they must descend the hill to the river, and follow the bank till they reached the general's gardens, where they would find a path direct to the house. Or, if they chose to go up hill, they would reach the general's barns half a verst from Miestetchki. It was this route they chose.

"But who is this von Rabbek?" asked one. "The man who commanded the N Cavalry Division at Plevna?"

"No, that was not von Rabbek, but simply Rabbe— without the von."

"What glorious weather!"

At the first barn they came to, two roads diverged; one ran straight forward and faded in the dusk; the other turning to the right led to the general's house. As the officers drew near they talked less loudly. To right and to left stretched rows of red-roofed brick barns, in aspect heavy and morose as the barracks of provincial towns. In front gleamed the lighted windows of von Rabbek's house.

"A good omen, gentlemen!" cried a young officer. "Our setter runs in advance. There is game ahead!"

On the face of Lieutenant Lobuitko, the tall stout officer referred to, there was not one trace of hair though he was twenty-five years old. He was famed among comrades for the instinct which told him of the presence of women in the neighbourhood. On hearing his comrade's remark, he turned his head and said—

"Yes. There are women there. My instinct tells me."

A handsome, well-preserved man of sixty, in mufti, came to the hall door to greet his guests. It was von Rabbek. As he pressed their hands, he explained that though he was delighted to see them, he must beg pardon for not asking them to spend the night; as guests he already had his two sisters, their children, his brother, and several neighbours—in fact, he had not one spare room. And though he shook their hands and apologised and smiled, it was plain that he was not half as glad to see them as was last year's Count, and that he had invited them merely because good manners demanded it. The officers climbing the soft-carpeted steps and listening to their host understood this perfectly well; and realised that they carried into the house an atmosphere of intrusion and alarm. Would any man—they asked themselves— who had gathered his two sisters and their children, his brother and his neighbours, to celebrate, no doubt, some family festival, find pleasure in the invasion of nineteen officers whom he had never seen before?

A tall elderly lady, with a good figure, and a long face with black eyebrows, who resembled closely the ex-Empress Eugenie, greeted them at the drawing-room door. Smiling courteously and with dignity, she affirmed that she was delighted to see the officers, and only regretted that she could not ask them to stay the night. But the courteous, dignified smile disappeared

when she turned away, and it was quite plain that she
had seen many officers in her day, that they caused not
the slightest interest, and that she had invited them
merely because an invitation was dictated by good
breeding and by her position in the world.

In a big dining-room seated at a big table sat ten
men and women, drinking tea. Behind them, veiled
in cigar-smoke, stood several young men, among them
one, red-whiskered and extremely thin, who spoke
English loudly with a lisp. Through an open door
the officers saw into a brightly lighted room with blue
wall-paper.

" You are too many to introduce singly, gentlemen ! "
said the general loudly, with affected joviality. " Make
one another's acquaintance, please—without formal-
ities ! "

The visitors, some with serious, even severe faces,
some smiling constrainedly, all with a feeling of awkwardness, bowed, and took their seats at the table.
Most awkward of all felt Staff-Captain Riabovitch, a
short, round-shouldered, spectacled officer, whiskered
like a lynx. While his brother officers looked serious
or smiled constrainedly, his face, his lynx whiskers, and
his spectacles seemed to explain: " I am the most
timid, modest, undistinguished officer in the whole
brigade." For some time after he took his seat at the
table he could not fix his attention on any single thing.
Faces, dresses, the cut-glass cognac bottles, the steaming

tumblers, the moulded cornices—all merged in a single, overwhelming sentiment which caused him intense fright and made him wish to hide his head. Like an inexperienced lecturer he saw everything before him, but could distinguish nothing, and was in fact the victim of what men of science diagnose as "psychical blindness."

But, slowly conquering his diffidence, Riabovitch began to distinguish and observe. As became a man both timid and unsocial, he remarked first of all the amazing temerity of his new friends. Von Rabbek, his wife, two elderly ladies, a girl in lilac, and the red-whiskered youth who, it appeared, was a young von Rabbek, sat down among the officers as unconcernedly as if they had held rehearsals, and at once plunged into various heated arguments in which they soon involved their guests. That artillerists have a much better time than cavalrymen or infantrymen was proved conclusively by the lilac girl, while von Rabbek and the elderly ladies affirmed the converse. The conversation became desultory. Riabovitch listened to the lilac girl fiercely debating themes she knew nothing about and took no interest in, and watched the insincere smiles which appeared on and disappeared from her face.

While the von Rabbek family with amazing strategy inveigled their guests into the dispute, they kept their eyes on every glass and mouth. Had every one tea, was it sweet enough, why didn't one eat biscuits, was another fond of cognac? And the longer Riabovitch listened and looked, the more pleased he was with this disingenuous, disciplined family.

, After tea the guests repaired to the drawing-room. Instinct had not cheated Lobuitko. The room was packed with young women and girls, and ere a minute had passed the setter-lieutenant stood beside a very young, fair-haired girl in black, and, bending down as if resting on an invisible sword, shrugged his shoulders coquettishly. He was uttering, no doubt, most unentertaining nonsense, for the fair girl looked indulgently at his sated face, and exclaimed indifferently, "Indeed!" And this indifferent "Indeed!" might have quickly convinced the setter that he was on a wrong scent.

Music began. As the notes of a mournful valse throbbed out of the open window, through the heads of all flashed the feeling that outside that window it was spring-time, a night of May. The air was odorous of young poplar leaves, of roses and lilacs —and the valse and the spring were sincere. Riabovitch, with valse and cognac mingling tipsily in his head, gazed at the window with a smile; then began to follow the movements of the women; and it seemed that the smell of roses, poplars, and lilacs came not from the gardens outside, but from the women's faces and dresses.

They began to dance. Young von Rabbek valsed

twice round the room with a very thin girl; and
Lobuitko, slipping on the parquetted floor, went up
to the girl in lilac, and was granted a dance.   But
Riabovitch stood near the door with the wall-flowers,
and looked silently on.   Amazed at the daring of
men who in sight of a crowd could take unknown
women by the waist, he tried in vain to picture
himself doing the same.   A time had been when he
envied his comrades their courage and dash, suffered
from painful heart-searchings, and was hurt by the
knowledge that he was timid, round-shouldered, and
undistinguished, that he had lynx whiskers, and that
his waist was much too long.   But with years he
had grown reconciled to his own insignificance, and
now looking at the dancers and loud talkers, he felt
no envy, but only mournful emotions.

At the first quadrille von Rabbek junior ap-
groached and invited two non-dancing officers to a
pame of billiards.   The three left the room; and
Riabovitch who stood idle, and felt impelled to join
in the general movement, followed.   They passed
the dining-room, traversed a narrow glazed corridor,
and a room where three sleepy footmen jumped from
a sofa with a start; and after walking, it seemed,
through a whole houseful of rooms, entered a small
billiard-room.

Von Rabbek and the two officers began their
game.   Riabovitch, whose only game was cards, stood

near the table and looked indifferently on, as the players, with unbuttoned coats, wielded their cues, moved about, joked, and shouted obscure technical terms. Riabovitch was ignored, save when one of the players jostled him or caught his cue, and turning towards him said briefly, "Pardon!", so that before the game was over he was thoroughly bored, and, impressed by a sense of his superfluity, resolved to return to the drawing-room, and turned away.

It was on the way back that his adventure took place. Before he had gone far he saw that he had missed his way. He remembered distinctly the room with the three sleepy footmen; and after passing through five or six rooms entirely vacant, he saw his mistake. Retracing his steps, he turned to the left, and found himself in an almost dark room which he had not seen before; and after hesitating a minute, he boldly opened the first door he saw, and found himself in complete darkness. Through a chink of the door in front peered a bright light; from afar throbbed the dulled music of a mournful mazurka. Here, as in the drawing-room, the windows were open wide, and the smell of poplars, lilacs, and roses flooded the air.

Riabovitch paused in irresolution. For a moment all was still. Then came the sound of hasty footsteps; then, without any warning of what was to come, a dress rustled, a woman's breathless voice

whispered "At last!", and two soft, scented, unmistakably womanly arms met round his neck, a
warm cheek impinged on his, and he received a
sounding kiss.   But hardly had the kiss echoed
through the silence when the unknown shrieked
loudly, and fled away—as it seemed to Riabovitch—
in disgust. Riabovitch himself nearly screamed, and
rushed headlong towards the bright beam in the
door-chink.

As he entered the drawing-room his heart beat
violently, and his hands trembled so perceptibly
that he clasped them behind his back.   His first
emotion was shame, as if every one in the room
already knew that he had just been embraced and
kissed. He retired into his shell, and looked fearfully
around. But finding that hosts and guests were calmly
dancing or talking, he regained courage, and surrendered himself to sensations experienced for the first
time in life.   The unexampled had happened.   His
neck, fresh from the embrace of two soft, scented arms,
seemed anointed with oil ; near his left moustache,
where the kiss had fallen, trembled a slight, delightful
chill, as from peppermint drops ; and from head to
foot he was soaked in new and extraordinary sensations, which continued to grow and grow.

He felt that he must dance, talk, run into the
garden, laugh unrestrainedly. He forgot altogether
that he was round-shouldered, undistinguished, lynx-

whiskered, that he had an "indefinite exterior"—
a description from the lips of a woman he had
happened to overhear. As Madame von Rabbek
passed him he smiled so broadly and graciously that
she came up and looked at him questioningly.

"What a charming house you have!" he said,
straightening his spectacles.

And Madame von Rabbek smiled back, said that
the house still belonged to her father, and asked were
his parents alive, how long he had been in the Army,
and why he was so thin. After hearing his answers
she departed. But though the conversation was over,
he continued to smile benevolently, and think what
charming people were his new acquaintances.

At supper Riabovitch ate and drank mechanically
what was put before him, heard not a word of the
conversation, and devoted all his powers to the un-
ravelling of his mysterious, romantic adventure.
What was the explanation? It was plain that one
of the girls, he reasoned, had arranged a meeting in
the dark room, and after waiting some time in vain
had, in her nervous tension, mistaken Riabovitch for
her hero. The mistake was likely enough, for on
entering the dark room Riabovitch had stopped
irresolutely as if he, too, were waiting for some one.
So far the mystery was explained.

"But which of them was it?" he asked, searching
the women's faces. She certainly was young, for old

women do not indulge in such romances. Secondly, she was not a servant. That was proved unmistakably by the rustle of her dress, the scent, the voice . . .

When at first he looked at the girl in lilac she pleased him; she had pretty shoulders and arms, a clever face, a charming voice. Riabovitch piously prayed that it was she. But, smiling insincerely, she wrinkled her long nose, and that at once gave her an elderly air. So Riabovitch turned his eyes on the blonde in black. The blonde was younger, simpler, sincerer; she had charming kiss-curls, and drank from her tumbler with inexpressible grace. Riabovitch hoped it was she—but soon he noticed that her face was flat, and bent his eyes on her neighbour.

"It is a hopeless puzzle," he reflected. "If you take the arms and shoulders of the lilac girl, add the blonde's curls, and the eyes of the girl on Lobuitko's left, then——"

He composed a portrait of all these charms, and had a clear vision of the girl who had kissed him. But she was nowhere to be seen.

Supper over, the visitors, sated and tipsy, bade their entertainers good-bye. Both host and hostess again apologised for not asking them to spend the night.

"I am very, very glad, gentlemen!" said the

general, and this time seemed to speak sincerely, no doubt because speeding the parting guest is a kindlier office than welcoming him unwelcomed. "I am very glad indeed! I hope you will visit me on your way back. Without ceremony, please! Which way will you go? Up the hill? No, go down the hill and through the garden. That way is shorter."

The officers took his advice. After the noise and glaring illumination within doors, the garden seemed dark and still. Until they reached the wicket-gate all kept silence. Merry, half tipsy, and content, as they were, the night's obscurity and stillness inspired pensive thoughts. Through their brains, as through Riabovitch's, sped probably the same question: "Will the time ever come when I, like von Rabbek, shall have a big house, a family, a garden, the chance of being gracious — even insincerely — to others, of making them sated, tipsy, and content?"

But once the garden lay behind them, all spoke at once, and burst into causeless laughter. The path they followed led straight to the river, and then ran beside it, winding around bushes, ravines, and over-hanging willow-trees. The track was barely visible; the other bank was lost entirely in gloom. Sometimes the black water imaged stars, and this was the only indication of the river's speed. From beyond it sighed a drowsy snipe, and beside them in a bush, heedless of the crowd, a nightingale chanted loudly. The officers gathered in a group, and swayed the bush, but the nightingale continued his song.

"I like his cheek!" they echoed admiringly. "He doesn't care a kopeck! The old rogue!"

Near their journey's end the path turned up the hill, and joined the road not far from the church enclosure; and there the officers, breathless from climbing, sat on the grass and smoked. Across the river gleamed a dull red light, and for want of a subject they argued the problem, whether it was a bonfire, a window-light, or something else. Riabovitch looked also at the light, and felt that it smiled and winked at him as if it knew about the kiss.

On reaching home, he undressed without delay, and lay upon his bed. He shared the cabin with Lobuitko and a Lieutenant Merzliakoff, a staid, silent little man, by repute highly cultivated, who took with him everywhere *The Messenger of Europe*, and read it eternally. Lobuitko undressed, tramped impatiently from corner to corner, and sent his servant for beer. Merzliakoff lay down, balanced the candle on his pillow, and hid his head behind *The Messenger of Europe*.

"Where is she now?" muttered Riabovitch, looking at the soot-blacked ceiling.

His neck still seemed anointed with oil, near his mouth still trembled the speck of pepperment chill. Through his brain twinkled successively the shoulders

and arms of the lilac girl, the kiss-curls and honest
eyes of the girl in black, the waists, dresses, brooches.
But though he tried his best to fix these vagrant
images, they glimmered, winked, and dissolved; and
as they faded finally into the vast black curtain
which hangs before the closed eyes of all men, he
began to hear hurried footsteps, the rustle of petti-
coats, the sound of a kiss. A strong, causeless joy
possessed him. But as he surrendered himself to this
joy, Lobuitko's servant returned with the news that
no beer was obtainable. The lieutenant resumed his
impatient march up and down the room.

"The fellow's an idiot," he exclaimed, stopping
first near Riabovitch and then near Merzliakoff.
"Only the worst numbskull and blockhead can't get
beer! *Canaille!*"

"Every one knows there's no beer here," said
Merzliakoff, without lifting his eyes from *The Messenger of Europe*.

"You believe that!" exclaimed Lobuitko. "Lord
in heaven, drop me on the moon, and in five minutes
I'll find both beer and women! I will find them
myself! Call me a rascal if I don't!"

He dressed slowly, silently lighted a cigarette, and
went out.

"Babbek, Grabbek, Labbek," he muttered, stopping
in the hall. "I won't go alone, devil take me! Riabovitch, come for a walk! What?"

As he got no answer, he returned, undressed slowly, and lay down.   Merzliakoff sighed, dropped the *Messenger of Europe*, and put out the light.   "Well?" muttered Lobuitko, puffing his cigarette in the dark.

Riabovitch pulled the bed-clothes up to his chin, curled himself into a roll, and strained his imagination to join the twinkling images into one coherent whole.   But the vision fled him.   He soon fell asleep, and his last impression was that he had been caressed and gladdened, that into his life had crept something strange, and indeed ridiculous, but uncommonly good and radiant.   And this thought did not forsake him even in his dreams.

When he awoke the feeling of anointment and peppermint chill were gone.   But joy, as on the night before, filled every vein.   He looked entranced at the window-panes gilded by the rising sun, and listened to the noises outside.   Some one spoke loudly under the very window.   It was Lebedietsky, commander of his battery, who had just overtaken the brigade.   He was talking to the sergeant-major, loudly, owing to lack of practice in soft speech.

"And what next?" he roared.

"During yesterday's shoeing, your honour, *Golubtchik* was pricked.   The *feldscher* ordered clay and vinegar.   And last night, your honour, mechanic Artemieff was drunk, and the lieutenant ordered him to be put on the limber of the reserve gun-carriage."

The sergeant-major added that Karpoff had forgotten the tent-pegs and the new lanyards for the friction-tubes, and that the officers had spent the evening at General von Rabbek's. But here at the window appeared Lebedietsky's red-bearded face. He blinked his short-sighted eyes at the drowsy men in bed, and greeted them.

"Is everything all right?"

"The saddle wheeler galled his withers with the new yoke," answered Lobuitko.

The commander sighed, mused a moment, and shouted—

"I am thinking of calling on Alexandra Yegorovna. I want to see her. Good-bye! I will catch you up before night."

Fifteen minutes later the brigade resumed its march. As he passed von Rabbek's barns Riabovitch turned his head and looked at the house. The venetian blinds were down; evidently all still slept. And among them slept she—she who had kissed him but a few hours before. He tried to visualise her asleep. He projected the bedroom window opened wide with green branches peering in, the freshness of the morning air, the smell of poplars, lilacs, and roses, the bed, a chair, the dress which rustled last night, a pair of tiny slippers, a ticking watch on the table—all these came to him clearly with every detail. But the features, the kind, sleepy smile—all, in

c

short, that was essential and characteristic—fled his
imagination as quicksilver flees the hand. When he
had covered half a verst he again turned back.
The yellow church, the house, gardens, and river
were bathed in light.   Imaging an azure sky, the
green-banked river specked with silver sunshine flakes
was inexpressibly fair; and, looking at Miestetchki
for the last time, Riabovitch felt sad, as if parting
for ever with something very near and dear.

By the road before him stretched familiar, uninteresting scenes; to the right and left, fields of young
rye and buckwheat with hopping rooks; in front,
dust and the napes of human necks; behind, the
same dust and faces. Ahead of the column marched
four soldiers with swords—that was the advance guard.
Next came the bandsmen.   Advance guard and bandsmen, like mutes in a funeral procession, ignored the
regulation intervals and marched too far ahead.   Riabovitch, with the first gun of Battery No. 5, could
see four batteries ahead.

To a layman, the long, lumbering march of an
artillery brigade is novel, interesting, inexplicable.
It is hard to understand why a single gun needs so
many men; why so many, such strangely harnessed
horses are needed to drag it.   But to Riabovitch, a
master of all these things, it was profoundly dull.
He had learned years ago why a solid sergeant-major
rides beside the officer in front of each battery;

why the sergeant-major is called the *unomi*, and why the drivers of leaders and wheelers ride behind him. Riabovitch knew why the near horses are called saddle-horses, and why the off horses are called led-horses—and all of this was uninteresting beyond words. On one of the wheelers rode a soldier still covered with yesterday's dust, and with a cumbersome, ridiculous guard on his right leg. But Riabovitch, knowing the use of this leg-guard, found it in no way ridiculous. The drivers, mechanically and with occasional cries, flourished their whips. The guns in themselves were unimpressive: The limbers were packed with tarpaulin-covered sacks of oats; and the guns themselves, hung round with tea-pots and satchels, looked like harmless animals, guarded for some obscure reason by men and horses. In the lee of the gun tramped six gunners, swinging their arms; and behind each gun came more *unosniye*, leaders, wheelers; and yet more guns, each as ugly and uninspiring as the one in front. And as every one of the six batteries in the brigade had four guns, the procession stretched along the road at least half a verst. It ended with a waggon train, with which, its head bent in thought, walked the donkey Magar, brought from Turkey by a battery commander.

Dead to his surroundings, Riabovitch marched onward, looking at the napes ahead or at the faces behind. Had it not been for last night's event, he would have been half asleep. But now he was absorbed in novel, entrancing thoughts. When the brigade set out that morning he had tried to argue that the kiss had no significance save as a trivial though mysterious adventure; that it was without real import; and that to think of it seriously was to behave himself absurdly. But logic soon flew away and surrendered him to his vivid imaginings. At times he saw himself in von Rabbek's dining-room, *tête-à-tête* with a composite being, formed of the girl in lilac and the blonde in black. At times he closed his eyes, and pictured himself with a different, this time quite an unknown, girl of cloudy feature; he spoke to her, caressed her, bent over her shoulder; he imagined war and parting . . . then reunion, the first supper together, children. . . .

"To the brakes!" rang the command as they topped the brow of each hill.

Riabovitch also cried "To the brakes!" and each time dreaded that the cry would break the magic spell, and recall him to realities.

They passed a big country house. Riabovitch looked across the fence into the garden, and saw a long path, straight as a ruler, carpeted with yellow sand, and shaded by young birches. In an ecstasy of enchantment, he pictured little feminine feet treading the yellow sand; and, in a flash, imagination restored the woman who had kissed him, the woman he had visualised after supper the night before. The image settled in his brain and never afterwards forsook him.

The spell reigned until midday, when a loud command came from the rear of the column.

"Attention! Eyes right! Officers!"

In a *calèche* drawn by a pair of white horses appeared the general of brigade. He stopped at the second battery, and called out something which no one understood. Up galloped several officers, among them Riabovitch.

"Well, how goes it?" The general blinked his red eyes, and continued, "Are there any sick?"

Hearing the answer, the little skinny general mused a moment, turned to an officer, and said—

"The driver of your third-gun wheeler has taken off his leg-guard and hung it on the limber. *Canaille!* Punish him!"

Then raising his eyes to Riabovitch, he added—

"And in your battery, I think, the harness is too loose."

Having made several other equally tiresome remarks, he looked at Lobuitko, and laughed.

"Why do you look so downcast, Lieutenant Lobuitko? You are sighing for Madame Lopukhoff, eh? Gentlemen, he is pining for Madame Lopukhoff!"

Madame Lopukhoff was a tall, stout lady, long

past forty. Being partial to big women, regardless
of age, the general ascribed the same taste to his
subordinates. The officers smiled respectfully; and
the general, pleased that he had said something
caustic and laughable, touched the coachman's back
and saluted. The *calèche* whirled away.

"All this, though it seems to me impossible and
unearthly, is in reality very commonplace," thought
Riabovitch, watching the clouds of dust raised by the
general's carriage. "It is an everyday event, and
within every one's experience. . . . This old general,
for instance, must have loved in his day; he is married now, and has children. Captain Wachter is also
married, and his wife loves him, though he has an
ugly red neck and no waist. . . . Salmanoff is
coarse, and a typical Tartar, but he has had a romance
ending in marriage. . . . I, like the rest, must go
through it all sooner or later."

And the thought that he was an ordinary man, and
that his life was ordinary, rejoiced and consoled him.
He boldly visualised *her* and his happiness, and let
his imagination run mad.

Towards evening the brigade ended its march.
While the other officers sprawled in their tents,
Riabovitch, Merzliakoff, and Lobuitko sat round a
packing-case and supped. Merzliakoff ate slowly,
and, resting the *Messenger of Europe* on his knees,
read on steadily. Lobuitko, chattering without cease,

poured beer into his glass. But Riabovitch, whose
head was dizzy from uninterrupted day-dreams, ate in
silence. When he had drunk three glasses he felt
tipsy and weak; and an overmastering impulse forced
him to relate his adventure to his comrades.

"A most extraordinary thing happened to me at
von Rabbek's," he began, doing his best to speak in
an indifferent, ironical tone. "I was on my way,
you understand, from the billiard-room. . . ."

And he attempted to give a very detailed history
of the kiss. But in a minute he had told the whole
story. In that minute he had exhausted every detail;
and it seemed to him terrible that the story required
such a short time. It ought, he felt, to have lasted
all the night. As he finished, Lobuitko, who as a
liar himself believed in no one, laughed incredulously.
Merzliakoff frowned, and, with his eyes still glued to
the *Messenger of Europe*, said indifferently—

"God knows who it was! She threw herself on
your neck, you say, and didn't cry out! Some lunatic,
I expect!"

"It must have been a lunatic," agreed Riabovitch.

"I, too, have had adventures of that kind," began
Lobuitko, making a frightened face. "I was on my
way to Kovno. I travelled second class. The carriage
was packed, and I couldn't sleep. So I gave the
guard a rouble, and he took my bag, and put me in
a *coupé*. I lay down, and pulled my rug over me.

It was pitch dark, you understand. Suddenly I felt some one tapping my shoulder and breathing in my face. I stretched out my hand, and felt an elbow. Then I opened my eyes. Imagine! A woman! Coal-black eyes, lips red as good coral, nostrils breathing passion, breasts—buffers!"

"Draw it mild!" interrupted Merzliakoff in his quiet voice. "I can believe about the breasts, but if it was pitch dark how could you see the lips?"

By laughing at Merzliakoff's lack of understanding, Lobuitko tried to shuffle out of the dilemma. The story annoyed Riabovitch. He rose from the box, lay on his bed, and swore that he would never again take any one into his confidence.

Life in camp passed without event. The days flew by, each like the one before. But on every one of these days Riabovitch felt, thought, and acted as a man in love. When at daybreak his servant brought him cold water, and poured it over his head, it flashed at once into his half-awakened brain that something good and warm and caressing had crept into his life.

At night when his comrades talked of love and of women, he drew in his chair, and his face was the face of an old soldier who talks of battles in which he has taken part. And when the rowdy officers, led by setter Lobuitko, made Don Juanesque raids upon the neighbouring "suburb," Riabovitch, though he accompanied them, was morose and conscience-struck, and mentally asked *her* forgiveness. In free hours and sleepless nights, when his brain was obsessed by memories of childhood, of his father, his mother, of everything akin and dear, he remembered always Miestetchki, the dancing horse, von Rabbek, von Rabbek's wife, so like the ex-Empress Eugenie, the dark room, the chink in the door.

On the thirty-first of August he left camp, this time not with the whole brigade but with only two batteries. As an exile returning to his native land, he was agitated and enthralled by day-dreams. He longed passionately for the queer-looking horse, the church, the insincere von Rabbeks, the dark room; and that internal voice which cheats so often the love-lorn whispered an assurance that he should see *her* again. But doubt tortured him. How should he meet her? What must he say? Would she have forgotten the kiss? If it came to the worst—he consoled himself—if he never saw her again, he might walk once more through the dark room, and re-member. . . .

Towards evening the white barns and well-known church rose on the horizon. Riabovitch's heart beat wildly. He ignored the remark of an officer who rode by, he forgot the whole world, and he gazed greedily at the river glimmering afar, at the green roofs, at the dove-cote, over which fluttered birds, dyed golden by the setting sun.

As he rode towards the church, and heard again the quartermaster's raucous voice, he expected every second a horseman to appear from behind the fence and invite the officers to tea. . . . But the quarter-master ended his harangue, the officers hastened to the village, and no horseman appeared.

"When Rabbek hears from the peasants that we are back he will send for us," thought Riabovitch. And so assured was he of this, that when he entered the hut he failed to understand why his comrades had lighted a candle, and why the servants were preparing the samovar.

A painful agitation oppressed him. He lay on his bed. A moment later he rose to look for the horseman. But no horseman was in sight. Again he lay down; again he rose; and this time, impelled by restlessness, went into the street, and walked towards the church. The square was dark and deserted. On the hill stood three silent soldiers. When they saw Riabovitch they started and saluted, and he, returning their salute, began to descend the well-remembered path.

Beyond the stream, in a sky stained with purple, the moon slowly rose. Two chattering peasant women walked in a kitchen garden and pulled cabbage leaves; behind them their log cabins stood out black against the sky. The river bank was as it had been in May; the bushes were the same; things differed only in that the nightingale no longer sang, that it smelt no longer of poplars and young grass.

When he reached von Rabbck's garden Riabovitch peered through the wicket-gate. Silence and darkness reigned. Save only the white birch trunks and patches of pathway, the whole garden merged in a black, impenetrable shade. Riabovitch listened greedily, and gazed intent. For a quarter of an hour he loitered; then hearing no sound, and seeing no light, he walked wearily towards home.

He went down to the river. In front rose the general's bathing-box; and white towels hung on the rail of the bridge. He climbed on to the bridge and stood still; then, for no reason whatever, touched a towel. It was clammy and cold. He looked down at the river which sped past swiftly, murmuring almost inaudibly against the bathing-box piles. Near the left bank glowed the moon's ruddy reflection, overrun by ripples which stretched it, tore it in two, and, it seemed, would sweep it away as twigs and shavings are swept.

"How stupid! How stupid!" thought Riabovitch, watching the hurrying ripples. "How stupid everything is!"

Now that hope was dead, the history of the kiss, his impatience, his ardour, his vague aspirations and disillusion appeared in a clear light. It no longer seemed strange that the general's horseman had not come, and that he would never again see *her* who had kissed him by accident instead of another. On the contrary, he felt, it would be strange if he did ever see her again. . . .

The water flew past him, whither and why no one knew. It had flown past in May; it had sped a stream into a great river; a river, into the sea; it had floated on high in mist and fallen again in rain; it might be, the water of May was again speeding past under Riabovitch's eyes. For what purpose? Why?

And the whole world—life itself—seemed to Riabovitch an inscrutable, aimless mystification. . . . Raising his eyes from the stream and gazing at the sky, he recalled how Fate in the shape of an unknown woman had once caressed him; he recalled his summer fantasies and images—and his whole life seemed to him unnaturally thin and colourless and wretched. . . .

When he reached the cabin his comrades had disappeared. His servant informed him that all had set out to visit " General Fonrabbkin," who had sent a horseman to bring them. . . . For a moment Riabovitch's heart thrilled with joy. But that joy he extinguished. He cast himself upon his bed, and wroth with his evil fate, as if he wished to spite it, ignored the invitation.

VEROTCHKA

.

VEROTCHKA

IVAN ALEXEIEVITCH OGNEFF well remembers the August evening when he opened noisily the glazed hall door and went out on to the terrace. He wore a light cloak and a wide-brimmed straw hat—the very hat which now, beside his top-boots, lies in the dust underneath his bed. He remembers that he carried a heavy package of books and manuscripts, and that in his free hand was a stout stick.

In the doorway, holding up a lamp, stood his host, Kuznetsoff, aged and bald-headed, with his long grey beard, and his cotton jacket, white as snow. And Kuznetsoff smiled benevolently and nodded his head.

"Good-bye, old friend!" cried Ogneff.

Kuznetsoff laid the lamp on the hall table, and followed Ogneff to the terrace. The narrow shadows of the two men swept down the steps, and, crossing the flower-beds, swayed, and came to a stop with the heads silhouetted against the lime-trees.

"Good-bye, and yet once more, thank you, old friend," said Ogneff. "Thanks for your heartiness, your kindness, your love. . . . Never . . . never in my whole life shall I forget your goodness. . . . You have been so kind . . . and your daughter has been so kind . . . all of you have been so kind, so gay, so hearty. . . . So good, indeed, that I cannot express my gratitude."

Under stress of feeling, under influence of the parting glass, Ogneff's voice sounded like a seminarist's, and his feeling showed not only in his words but in the nervous twitching of eyes and shoulders. And Kuznetsoff, touched also by emotion and wine, bent over the young man and kissed him.

"I have grown as used to you as if I were your dog," continued Ogneff. "I have been with you day after day. I have spent the night at your house a dozen times, and drunk so much of your liqueurs that it frightens me to think of it. . . . But, most of all, Gavriil Petrovitch, I thank you for your co-operation and help. Without you, I should have been worrying over my statistics till October. But I will put in my preface: 'It is my duty to express to M. Kuznetsoff, President of the N. District Zemstvo Executive, my gratitude for his kind assistance.' Statistics have a brilliant future! Give my deepest regards to Vera Gavriilovna! And tell the doctors, the two magistrates, and your secretary that I shall never forget their kindness. . . . And now, old friend, let us embrace and kiss for the last time!"

Ogneff again kissed the old man. When he reached the last step, he turned his head and said—

"I wonder shall we ever meet again."

"God knows," answered Kuznetsoff. "Probably never."

"I fear so. Nothing will lure you to Peters-burg, and it is not likely that I shall ever return to these parts. Good-bye!"

"But leave your books," called Kuznetsoff after him. "Why carry such a weight? My man will bring them to-morrow."

But Ogneff, who had not heard him, walked quickly away. Warmed with wine, his heart was full at the same time of sorrow and joy. He walked forward reflecting how often in life we meet such kindly men and women, how sad it is that they leave but memories behind. It is as on a journey. The traveller sees on the flat horizon the outline of a crane; the weak wind bears its plaintive cry; yet in a moment it is gone; and strain his eyes as he may towards the blue distance, he sees no bird, and hears no sound. So in the affairs of men, faces and voices tremble a moment before us, and slip away into the gone-before, leaving behind them nothing but the vain records of memory. Having been every day at hearty Kuznetsoff's house since he arrived that spring at N., Ogneff had come to know and love as kinsmen the old man, his daughter, their servants.

D

He knew every spot in the old house, the cosy terrace, the turns in the garden paths, the trees outlined
against garden and bathing-box. And now in a few
seconds when he had passed the wicket-gate, all these
would be memories, void for evermore of real significance. A year—two years—would pass, and all
these kindly images, dulled beyond restoring, would
recur only in memory as the shapeless impressions of
a dream.

"In life," thought Ogneff, as he approached the
gate, "there is nothing better than men. Nothing!"

It was warm and still. The whole world smelt of
heliotropes, mignonette, and tobacco-plants which had
not yet shed their blooms. Around shrubs and tree-
trunks flowed a sea of thin, moonlight-soaked mist;
and—what long remained in Ogneff's memory—wisps
of vapour, white as ghosts, floated with motion
imperceptibly slow across the garden path. Near the
moon, shining high in heaven, swam transparent
patches of cloud. The whole world, it seemed, was
built of coal-black shadows and wandering wisps of
white; and, to Ogneff, it seemed as if he were looking
not at Nature, but at a decorated scene, as if clumsy
pyrotechnists, illuminating the garden with white Bengal fire, had flooded the air with a sea of snowy smoke.

As Ogneff approached the wicket-gate a black
shadow moved from the low palisade and came to
meet him.

"Vera Gavriilovna," he exclaimed joyfully. "You here! After I had looked for you everywhere to say good-bye! . . . Good-bye, I am going."

"So early—it is barely eleven o'clock."

"But late for me. I have a five-verst walk, and I must pack up to-night. I leave early to-morrow. . . ."

Before Ogneff stood Kuznetsoff's daughter, twenty-one-year-old Vera, whom he had seen so often, pensive and carelessly-dressed and interesting. Day-dreaming girls who spend whole days lying down or in desultory reading, who suffer from tedium and melancholy, usually dress without care. But if Nature has given them taste and the instinct of beauty, this negligence in dress has often a charm of its own. And, indeed, Ogneff, recalling the vision of pretty Vera, cannot imagine her without a loose jacket, hanging in folds away from her waist, without untidy curls on her forehead, without the red, shaggy-tasselled shawl which all day long lay in the hall among the men's caps, or on the chest in the dining-room, where the old cat used it unceremoniously as bed. The shawl and the creased jacket seemed to express the easy-going indolence of a sedentary life. But perhaps it was because Ogneff liked Vera, that every button and fold exhaled to him goodness and poetry, something foreign to women insincere, void of the instinct of beauty, and cold. . . . And Vera, too, had a good figure, regular features, and pretty wavy hair   To Ogneff, who knew few women, she seemed beautiful.

"I am going away," he said again, bidding her good-bye at the wicket-gate. "Think well of me! And thanks for everything!"

And again twitching his shoulders, and speaking in the sing-song seminarist's voice which he had used to the old man, he thanked Vera for her hospitality, her kindness, her heartiness.

"I wrote about you to my mother in every letter," he said. "If all men were like you and your father, life on earth would be paradise. Every one in your house is the same. So simple, so hearty, so sincere. . . ."

"Where are you going?"

"First to my mother, in Oriol. I shall spend two days there.   Then to St. Petersburg to work."

"And then?"

"Then? I shall work all winter, and in spring go somewhere in the country to collect material. Well . . . be happy, live a hundred years, and think well of me! This is the last time we meet."

Ogneff bowed his head and kissed Verotchka's hand; then in silent confusion straightened his cloak, rearranged his package of books, and said—

"What a thick mist to-night!"

"Yes. Have you not forgotten anything?"

"Nothing . . . I think."

For a moment Ogneff stood silently. Then he
turned awkwardly to the gate and went out of the
garden.

"Wait! Let me go with you as far as the wood,"
said Vera, running after him.

They followed the road. Trees no longer obscured
the view, and they could see the sky, and the country
far ahead. Through breaks in the veil of semi-
transparent smoke, the world exposed its fairness; the
white mist lay unevenly around bushes and hayricks,
or wandered in tiny cloudlets, clinging to the surface
as if not to cut off the view. The road could be
seen all the way to the wood, and in the ditches
beside it rose little bushes which trapped and hindered
the vagabond mist wisps. Half a verst away rose a
dark belt of forest.

"Why has she come? I shall have to see her
home," Ogneff asked himself. But looking at Vera's
profile, he smiled kindly, and said—

"I hate going away in weather like this. This
evening is quite romantic, what with the moonlight,
the silence . . . and all the honours! Do you know
what, Vera Gavriilovna? I am now twenty-nine years
old, yet have never had a single romance! In all
my life so far, not one! So of trysts, paths
of sighs, and kisses, I know only by hearsay. It is
abnormal. Sitting in my own room in town, I never
notice the void. But here in the open air I

somehow feel it . . . strongly . . . it is almost annoying."

"But what is the cause?"

"I can't say. Perhaps it is because so far I have never had time, perhaps simply because I have never yet met a woman who . . . But I have few friends, and seldom go anywhere."

They walked three hundred yards in silence. As Ogneff looked at Vera's shawl and uncovered head, he recalled the past spring and summer days, when far from his grey St. Petersburg rooms, caressed by kindly Nature and by kindly friends, pursuing his much-loved work, he had seen slip by, uncounted, sunset after dawn, day after day, nor noticed how, foreshadowing summer's end, the nightingale first, the quail, and then the corncrake ceased their songs. Time had passed unseen; and that, he supposed, meant that life had spun out pleasantly and without jar. He recalled how at the end of April he had arrived at N., a poor man, unused to society; and expected nothing but tedium, solitude, and contempt for statistics—which in his opinion took a high place among the useful sciences. He remembered the April evening of his arrival at the inn of Old-Believer Riabukhin, where for twenty kopecks a day he was given a bright, clean room, with only one restriction, that he should smoke out of doors. He remembered how he had rested a few hours, and, asking for the

address of the President of the Zemstvo Executive,
had set out on foot to Gavriil Petrovitch's house;
how he had tramped through four versts of rich
meadows and young plantations; how high under a
veil of cloud trembled a lark, filling the world with
silver sounds, while above the green pastures, with
a stolid, pompous flapping of wings, the rooks flew
up and down.

"Is it possible?" Ogneff asked himself, "that they
breathe this air every day, or is it perfumed only
this evening in honour of me?"

He remembered how, expecting a dry, business-like
reception, he had entered Kuznetsoff's study timidly,
with averted face, and shyly stroked his beard. And
how the old man contracted his brows, and failed
utterly to understand what this young man with his
statistics wanted with the Zemstvo Executive. But
as he began to understand what statistics really
mean, and how they are collected, Gavriil Petrovitch woke up, smiled, and with infantile curiosity
began to examine his visitor's note-books. . . .
And on the evening of the same day, Ogneff sat at
Kuznetsoff's supper-table, grew tipsy on strong liqueurs,
and, watching the placid faces and lazy gestures of
his new acquaintances, felt spreading through his
whole body that sweet, drowsy indolence of one who,
wanting to continue his sleep, stretches himself and
smiles. And his new-found friends looked at him

lovingly, asked were his father and mother alive, how much he earned a month, and whether he often went to the theatre.

Ogneff recalled the long drives through the cantons, the picnics, the fishing parties, the trip to the convent when the Mother Superior presented each visitor with a bead-purse; he recalled the endless, heated, truly Russian arguments in which the disputants, banging their fists on the table, misunderstood and interrupted without knowing what they meant to say, wandered from the subject, and after arguing fiercely a couple of hours, exclaimed with a laugh, "The devil knows what this dispute is about. We began about health, and are now arguing about rest in the grave!"

"Do you remember when you and I rode to Shestovo with the doctor?" asked Ogneff as they drew near to the wood. "We met a lunatic. I gave him five kopecks, and he crossed himself thrice, and threw the money in my face. What hosts of impressions I carry away—if fused in a compact mass, I should have a big ingot of gold! I never understood why clever, sensitive men crowd into big cities instead of living in the country. Is there more space and truth on the Nevsky, and in the big damp houses? My house, for instance, which is packed from top to bottom with artists, students, and journalists, always seems to me to embody an absurd prejudice."

Some twenty paces from the wood the road crossed a narrow bridge with posts at the corners. During their spring walks, this bridge was a stopping place for the Kuznetsoffs and their visitors. Thence they could draw echoes from the wood, and watch the road as it vanished in a black drive.

"We are at the bridge," said Ogneff. "You must return."

Vera stopped, and drew a deep breath.

"Let us sit down for a minute," she said, seating herself on a pillar. "When we say good-bye to friends we always sit down here."

Ogneff sat beside her on his parcel of books, and continued to speak. Vera breathed heavily, and looked straight into the distance, so that he could not see her face.

"Perhaps some day, in ten years' time, we'll meet somewhere again," he said. "Things will be different. You will be the honoured mother of a family, and I the author of a respectable, useless book of statistics, fat as forty thousand albums put together. . . . To-night, the present counts, it absorbs and agitates us. But ten years hence we shall remember neither the date nor the month, nor even the year, when we sat on this bridge together for the last time. You, of course, will be changed. You will change."

"What?"

"I asked you just now. . . ."

"I did not hear."

Only now did Ogneff notice the change that had come over Vera. She was pale and breathless; her hands and lips trembled; and instead of the usual single lock of hair falling on her forehead, there were two. She did her best to mask her agitation and avoid looking him in the face; and to help in this, she first straightened her collar as if it were cutting her neck, and then drew the red shawl from one side to the other.

"You are cold, I am afraid," began Ogneff. "You must not sit in the mist. Let me see you home."

Vera did not answer.

"What is the matter?" resumed Ogneff. "You do not answer my questions. You are ill?"

Vera pressed her hand firmly to her cheek, and suddenly drew it away.

"It is too awful," she whispered, with a look of intense agony. "Too awful!"

"What is too awful?" asked Ogneff, shrugging his shoulders, and making no attempt to conceal his surprise. "What is the matter?"

Still breathing heavily and twitching her shoulders, Vera turned away from him, and after looking a moment at the sky, began—

"I have to speak to you, Ivan Alexeievitch. . . ."

"I am listening."

"I know it will seem strange to you . . . you will be astonished, but I do not care. . . ."

Ogneff again shrugged his shoulders and prepared to listen.

"It is this . . . ," began Vera, averting her eyes, and twirling thé shawl-tassels in her fingers. "You see, this is . . . that is what I wanted to say. . . . It will seem absurd to you . . . and stupid . . . but I cannot bear it!"

Vera's words, half smothered in incoherent stammering, were suddenly interrupted by tears. She hid her face in the shawl, and wept bitterly. Ogneff, confused and stupefied, coughed, and, having no idea what to say or do, looked helplessly around. He was unused to tears, and Vera's breakdown seemed to make his own eyes water.

"Come, come!" he stammered helplessly. "Vera Gavriilovna! What does this mean? Are you ill? Some one has annoyed you? Tell me what it is . . . and perhaps I can help you."

And when, in a last attempt to console her, he drew her hands cautiously from her face, she smiled at him through her tears, and said—

"I . . . I love you!"

The words, simple and ordinary, were spoken in a simple and ordinary voice. But Ogneff, covered with intense confusion, turned his face away.

His confusion was followed by fright. The atmo-

sphere of mournfulness, warmth, and sentiment inspired
by liqueurs and leave-takings, suddenly made way for
a sharp, unpleasant feeling of awkwardness. Feeling
that his whole soul had been turned inside out, he
looked shyly at Vera; and she, having avowed her
love, and cast for ever away her woman's enhancing
inaccessibility, seemed smaller, simpler, meaner.

"What does it all mean?" he asked himself in
terror. "And then . . . do I love her . . . or
not?—that is the problem."

But she, now that the hardest, painfullest part was
ended, breathed easily and freely. She rose from her
seat, and, looking straight into Ogneff's eyes, spoke
quickly, warmly, without constraint.

Those who have been overtaken by sudden terror
seldom remember details, and Ogneff to-day recalls
not one of Vera's words. He remembers only their
import and the emotions they brought forth. He
remembers her voice, which seemed to come from a
strangled throat, a voice hoarse with emotion, and
the magic passion and harmony in its intonations.
Crying, smiling, scattering tear-drops from her eyes,
she confessed that since the first days of their friend-
ship she had been won by his originality, his intellect,
his kind, clever eyes, and by the aims and aspirations
of his life. That she loved him devoutly, passionately, madly; that in summer when she went from the
garden into the house and saw his coat in the hall, or

heard his voice, her heart thrilled with a presage of intense joy; that his most trivial jokes had made her laugh; that every figure in his note-books exhaled to her wisdom and majesty; that even his cane standing in the hall had seemed to her lovelier than the trees.

The wood, the patches of mist, even the black roadside ditches were charmed, it seemed, as they listened. But Ogneff's heart felt only estrangement and pain. Avowing her love, Vera was entrancingly fair; her words were noble and impassioned. But Ogneff felt not the pleasure or vital joy which he himself yearned for, but only sympathy with Vera, and pain that a fellow-creature should suffer so for his sake. Heaven only knows why it was so! But whether the cause was book-learned reason, or merely that impregnable objectivity which forbids some men to live as men, the ecstasy and passion of Vera seemed to him affected and unreal. Yet even while he felt this, something whispered that, in the light of Nature and personal happiness, that which he listened to then was a thousand times more vital than all his books, his statistics, his eternal verities. And he was angry, and reproached himself, though he had no idea wherein he was at fault.

What increased his confusion was that he knew he must reply. An answer was inevitable. To say to Vera plainly "I do not love you!" he had not the strength. But he could not say "I do," for with all his searchings he could not find in his heart a single spark.

And he listened silently while she said that she could know no greater happiness than to see him, to follow him, to go with him wheresoever he might go, to be his wife and helper . . . and that if he abandoned her she would die of grief.

"I cannot stay here," she exclaimed, wringing her hands. "I have come to detest this house, and this wood, and this air. I am tired of this changeless restfulness and aimless life; I can stand no longer our colourless, pale people, as like one another as two drops of water! They are genial and kind . . . because they are contented, because they have never suffered and never struggled. But I can stand it no more. . . . I want to go to the big grey houses, where people suffer, embittered by labour and need. . . ."

And all this seemed to Ogneff affected and unreal. When Vera ceased to speak he was still without an answer. But silence was impossible, and he stammered out—

"I . . . Vera Gavriilovna . . . I am very grateful to you, although I feel that I deserve no such . . . such feelings. In the second place, as an honest man, I must say that . . . happiness is based on mutuality . . . that is, when both parties . . . when they love equally."

Ogneff suddenly felt ashamed of his stammering

speech, and was silent. He felt that his expression was guilty, stupid, and dull, and that his face was strained and drawn out. And Vera, it seemed, could read the truth in his looks, for she paled, looked at him with terror, and averted her eyes.

"You will forgive me," stammered Ogneff, feeling the silence past bearing. "I respect you so very, very much that . . . that I am sorry . . ."

Vera suddenly turned away, and walked rapidly towards the house. Ogneff followed her.

"No, there is no need!" she said, waving her hand. "Do not come! I will go alone. . . ."

"But still . . . I must see you home."

All that Ogneff had said, even his last words, seemed to him flat and hateful. The feeling increased with each step. He raged at himself and, clenching his fists, cursed his coldness and awkwardness with women. In a last vain effort to stir his own feelings he looked at Vera's pretty figure, at her hair, at the imprints of her little feet on the dusty road. He remembered her words and her tears. But all this filled him only with pain, and left his feelings dead.

"Yes. . . . A man cannot force himself to love!" he reasoned, and at the same time thought, "When shall I ever love except by force? I am nearly thirty. Better than Verotchka among women I have never met . . . and never shall meet. Oh, accursed old age! Old age at thirty!"

Vera walked before him, each moment quickening her steps. Her face was bowed to the ground, and she did not look round once. It seemed to Ogneff that she had suddenly grown slighter and that her shoulders were narrower.

"I can imagine her feelings," he said to himself. "Shame . . . and such pain as to make her wish for death! . . . And in her words there was life and poetry, and meaning enough to have melted a stone! But I . . . I am senseless and blind."

"Listen, Vera Gavriilovna." This cry burst from him against his will. "You must not think that I . . . that I . . ."

Ogneff hesitated and said nothing more. At the wicket-gate Vera turned, looked at him for an instant, and, wrapping her shawl tightly around her shoulders, walked quickly up the path.

Ogneff remained alone. He turned back to the wood, and walked slowly, stopping now and then and looking towards the gate. His movements expressed doubt of himself. He searched the road for the imprints of Verotchka's feet. He refused to credit that one whom he liked so much had avowed to him her love, and that he had awkwardly, boorishly scorned her. For the first time in life he realised how little one's actions depend from mere goodwill; and he felt as feels every honourable, kindly man who, despite his intentions, has caused his nearest and dearest unmeant and unmerited suffering.

His conscience stung him. When Verotchka vanished in the garden he felt that he had lost something very dear which he would never find again. With Vera, it seemed to him, a part of his youth had passed away, and he knew that the precious moments he had let slip away without profit would never return.

When he reached the bridge he stopped in thought, and sought the cause of his unnatural coldness. That it lay not outside himself, but within, he saw clearly. And he frankly confessed that this was not the rational calmness boasted by clever men, not the coldness of inflated egoism, but simply impotence of soul, dull insensibility to all that is beautiful, old age before its day—the fruit, perhaps, of his training, his grim struggle for bread, his friendless, bachelor life.

He walked slowly, as if against his own will, from the bridge to the wood. There where on a pall of impenetrable black the moonlight shone in jagged patches he remained alone with his thoughts; and he passionately longed to regain all that he had lost.

And Ogneff remembers that he returned to the house. Goading himself forward with memories of what had passed, straining his imagination to paint Vera's face, he walked quickly as far as the garden.

E

From road and garden the mist had melted away, and a bright, newly washed moon looked down from an unflecked sky; the east alone frowned with clouds. Ogneff remembers his cautious steps, the black windows, the drowsy scent of heliotropes and mignonette. He remembers how old friend Karpo, wagging genially his tail, came up and snuffed at his hand. But no other living thing did he see. He remembers how he walked twice around the house, stood awhile before the black window of Vera's room; and abandoning his quest with a sigh returned to the road.

An hour later he was back in town; and, weary, broken, leaning his body and hot face against the gate, knocked at the inn. In the distance barked a sleepy dog; and the night watchman at the church beat an iron shield.

"Still gadding about at night!" grumbled the Old-Believer, as in a long, woman's night-dress he opened the door. "What do you gain by it? It would be better for you if you stayed at home and prayed to God!"

When he entered his room Ogneff threw himself upon the bed, and long gazed steadily at the fire. At last he rose, shook his head, and began to pack his trunk.

ON TRIAL

ON TRIAL

IN the district capital N. stands a brown Government building, used in turn by the Zemstvo Executive, the Session of Justices, the Peasant, Licensing, Recruiting, and many other local authorities; and here, on a dull autumn day, were held the district assizes.

This was the brown building of which a local official joked: "It's the seat of justice, of the police, of the militia—in fact, quite an institute for young gentlewomen."

In confirmation of the proverb that too many cooks spoil the broth, this brown building makes a bad impression on the unofficial man by its gloomy barrack-like view, its air of decay, and by the entire absence of even a pretence to comfort, without or within. Even on glaring spring days it is oppressed by deep shadows; and on bright moonlight nights, when trees and houses, blending in one thick shade, repose in deep gloom, it squats alone like a dumpy stone, crushing and out of place, on the modest landscape, spoils the harmony of its neighbours, and breathes an irritable restlessness, as if tortured by memories of past, unforgiven sins. Inside, it is a barn, painfully comfortless. It is strange indeed how these fastidious procurators, judges, marshals of the nobility who at home make scenes over a smoking chimney or a stain on the floor, are reconciled here with the humming ventilators, the sickening smell of wax matches, and the dirty, damp-spotted walls.

When at nine o'clock the court assembled trials began with unusual haste. Case after case ended quickly, "as a church service without hymns"; and no one reaped a single picturesque impression from the hurried, heterogeneous procession of men, movements, speeches, misfortunes, truths, falsehoods. By two o'clock much work had been done: two men condemned to punitive regiments, one criminal of the privileged classes deprived of his rights and sent to gaol, one prisoner acquitted, and one case postponed.

At two o'clock the President announced the trial of Nikolai Kharlamoff on the charge of murdering his wife. The court was constituted as during the earlier cases. The counsel for the accused was a new barrister —a young, beardless "Candidate" in a frock-coat with bright buttons.

"Bring in the accused!" cried the President.

But the accused was already on his way to the dock. He was a tall, sturdy peasant, aged fifty-five, bald, with an apathetic, hairy face, and a great carroty beard.

Behind him marched a little insignificant soldier armed
with a rifle.

Almost at the door of the dock an accident happened to this soldier. He slipped suddenly, and his
rifle flew from his hand. Before it touched the floor
he caught it, but knocked his knee sharply against
the butt. Whether from pain or from confusion at
his awkwardness, the soldier turned very red.

There was the usual questioning of the accused,
assembling of jurymen, counting and swearing of witnesses. The indictment was read. A narrow-shouldered,
pale secretary, much too thin for his uniform, with
sticking-plaster on his cheek, read quickly in a low
thick bass, which, as if fearing to injure his chest, he
neither raised nor lowered; as accompaniment, the
ventilators hummed tirelessly behind the judges'
bench; and the general result was a chorus which
broke on the silence of the room with drowsy, narcotic
effect.

The presiding judge, a short-sighted, middle-aged
man with a look of extreme fatigue, sat motionless,
and held his hand to his forehead as if shading his
eyes from the sun. While the ventilator hummed and
the secretary droned, he was thinking of something
not connected with work. When the secretary paused
to take breath and turn over a page, he started suddenly, and, bending to the ear of his colleague, asked
with a sigh—

" Are you staying at Demianoff's, Matvei Petrovitch ? "

" Yes, Demianoff's," was the reply, also given with
a start.

" Next time I will stay there too.   Tipiakoff's is
absolutely unendurable.   Noise and uproar all night !
Tapping, coughing, crying children.   It's unbearable ! "

The assistant procurator, a stout, sated brunet, with
gold spectacles and a neatly trimmed beard, sat motionless as a statue, and, resting his face on his hand, read
Byron's *Cain*.   His eyes expressed greedy absorption,
and his brows rose higher and higher.   Sometimes
he lay back in his chair and looked indifferently ahead,
but soon again became absorbed in his book.   The
defending advocate drew a blunt pencil along the
table, and, his head inclined aside, thought.   His
young face expressed only concentrated, cold tedium,
such tedium as shows on the faces of schoolboys and
clerks who sit day after day in the same places and
see the same people and the same walls.   The speech
he was to make in no way troubled him.   And, indeed,
what was it ?   By command of his senior it would
follow a long-established convention ; and, conscious
that it was colourless and tiresome, without passion
or fire, he would blurt it out to the jurymen, then
gallop away through rain and mud to the railway
station, thence to town, where he would be sent some-

where else in the district to make another stupid speech. It was tiresome!

At first the prisoner coughed nervously and paled. But soon even he succumbed to the all-pervading calm, monotony, and tedium. Glancing with dull respect at the judges' uniforms and the jurymen's tired faces, he blinked his eyes indifferently. The legal atmosphere and procedure, fear of which had so tortured him in gaol, acted now as a sedative. Nothing fulfilled his expectations. He had come into court charged of murder; yet he found no threatening faces, no indignant gestures, no loud phrases about justice, no interest in his uncommon lot; not even his judges turned on him a long and searching glance. The dark windows, the walls, the secretary's voice, the procurator's pose—all were soaked with official indifference and exhaled a chill. It seemed as if a murderer were a simple office accessory, as if he were to be judged not by living men, but by some invisible machine, brought God knows whence.

The narcotised peasant did not understand that his judges were as used to the dramas and tragedies of life as hospital doctors are to death, and that it was just in this mechanical impartiality that lay the terror, the hopelessness of his case. For if, instead of sitting still, he had risen and begun to implore, to shed tears for mercy, to repent bitterly, to die of despair—all would have fallen as vainly upon numbed nerves and custom as waves upon a rock.

The indictment was finished. The President aimlessly stroked the table before him, blinked his eyes at the prisoner, and asked, idly rolling his tongue—

"Prisoner at the bar, do you confess to the murder of your wife on the evening of the 9th of July?"

"I am not guilty," answered the accused man, rising, and holding the breast of his *khalat.*

The Court hurriedly set about the examination of witnesses, and soon had questioned two peasant women, five men, and the detective charged with the investigation of the crime. All of these, splashed with mud, fatigued with walking and waiting in the witnesses' room, melancholy and morose, told the same tale. Kharlamoff, they agreed, lived with his wife "well," and beat her only when he was drunk. At sunset on the 9th of July the old woman was found in the shed attached to her cabin with her skull beaten in. Beside her in a pool of blood lay a hatchet. When they looked for Kharlamoff to tell him of the tragedy he was neither in the hut nor in the street. They looked for him about the village, searched the drink-shops and huts, but he had vanished. Two days later he appeared at the office, pale, tattered, trembling all over. He was handcuffed and locked up.

"Prisoner!" The President turned to Kharlamoff.

"Can you not explain to the court where you spent the two days after the murder?"

"I tramped the country. . . . I had nothing to eat or drink. . . ."

"But if you were innocent why did you hide yourself?"

"I was afraid. . . . I thought I might be accused."

"I see. . . . Very good. Sit down!"

The district physician who examined the woman's body was the last witness. He told the court all that he remembered out of the post-mortem protocol; and added what he had reasoned out on the way to the trial. The President blinked at the witness's new, shiny black coat, his fashionable necktie, his moving lips; and through his head ran the idle thought, "Every one wears short coats nowadays? Why is his cut long? Why long, and not short?"

Behind the President, boots creaked cautiously. The assistant procurator had come to the table to fetch a paper.

"Mikhail Vladimirovitch!" The assistant procurator bent down to the President's ear. "This Koreisky has investigated the case with incredible carelessness. The man's brother was not even questioned; and you can't make head or tail of the description of the hut. . . ."

"What can you do? . . . What can you do?" sighed the President, leaning back in his chair.

"By the by," resumed the assistant procurator; "look, there in the hall, the first bench . . . the man with the actor's face. That is the local money magnate. He has about half a million in ready cash."

"Indeed! He doesn't look it. . . . Well, old man, shall we have an interval?"

"Let's finish the case, and then. . . ."

"How do you know? . . ." The President turned to the doctor. "So you find that death was immediate?"

"Yes, as the result of serious injury to the substance of the brain. . . ."

When the doctor finished, the President looked at the blank space between procurator and defending counsel and asked: "Have you any questions to put?"

The assistant procurator without lifting his eyes from *Cain* shook his head. The defending counsel moved brusquely, coughed, and asked—

"Tell me, doctor, judging by the size of the wound, could you form any judgment as to . . . as to the murderer's mental condition? That is, I want to know if the size of the wound justifies our concluding that the accused was in an epileptic fit."

The President turned his sleepy, indifferent glance on the defending counsel. The procurator raised his eyes from *Cain* and looked at the President. But it was a mere look, expressing neither amusement nor surprise, expressing, in fact, nothing at all.

The doctor hesitated. "If you consider the force with which the accused delivered the blow. . . . Otherwise . . . But excuse me, I do not quite understand your point."

The defending lawyer got no answer to his question, and, indeed, needed none. He knew that it had arisen in his mind, and flowed from his lips, merely under the spell of the tedium, the stillness, the humming ventilators. Releasing the doctor, the court examined the articles produced as evidence. First they looked at a caftan, on the sleeve of which was a dark brown spot of blood. The origin of this spot was explained by Kharlamoff as follows—

"Three days before my wife's death Penkoff bled his horse. I was there, and, of course, helped him . . . and I got smeared with blood. . . ."

"But Penkoff has just sworn that he does not remember you being present when the horse was bled."

"I do not know. . . ."

"Sit down."

The court examined the hatchet found beside the dead woman.

"That is not my hatchet," said the accused.

"Whose, then?"

"I do not know . . . I had no hatchet."

"No peasant can carry on his business without a hatchet. Your neighbour, Ivan Timofeitch, who mended the sledge with you, swears that the hatchet is yours. . . ."

"I know nothing . . . only this, that I swear before God"—Kharlamoff extended his hand and opened wide his fingers—"I swear before my true Creator . . . I cannot even remember when I last had a hatchet. I once had one like that, only a little smaller, but my son Proshka lost it. About two years before he was taken as a soldier he went to cut wood—he went playing with the children, and lost it. . . ."

"That will do. Sit down!"

The persistent distrust and unwillingness of all to listen at last irritated and enraged Kharlamoff. He blinked his eyes furiously, and on his cheek-bones appeared two bright red spots.

"Before the eyes of God!" he exclaimed, stretching out his hand. "If you do not believe me, then ask my son Proshka!" He spoke in a rough voice, and turned suddenly to the little soldier who guarded him. "Proshka, where is the hatchet? Where is the hatchet?"

It was a terrible moment. All in court, it seemed, sank into their seats and dwindled to points. . . . Through every head like lightning flashed one and the same terrible thought, and not one out of all of them dared to look at the soldier's face. Each did his best to discredit his own ears, to cherish the delusion that he had not heard aright.

"Prisoner, you are not allowed to speak to the guard!" said the President hastily.

No one saw the soldier's face, and terror flew through the court unseen. The usher rose from his bench, and on tiptoes, swinging his arms, went out of the hall. In half a minute came the sound of dull footfalls and such noises as are heard when sentries are relieved.

All raised their heads and, trying to look as if nothing uncommon had happened, continued their work. . . .

THE MASS FOR THE DEAD

THE MASS FOR THE DEAD

AT the church of the Odigitrieff Virgin in Verch-niye Zaprudni village the service had just ended. The worshippers moved from their places and left the church; and soon no one remained save the shopkeeper, Andrei Andreitch, one of the oldest residents, and a member of the local "Intelligentsia." Andrei Andreitch leaned on his elbow on the rail of the choir and waited. On his face, well shaven, fat, and marked with traces of old pimples, were two inimical expressions: resignation to inscrutable destiny, and unlimited, dull contempt for his fellow-worshippers in their cheap overcoats and gaudy handkerchiefs. As it was Sunday, he was dressed in his best. He wore a cloth overcoat with yellow bone buttons, blue trousers outside his top-boots, and solid goloshes, such big, awkward goloshes as are worn only by people positive, deliberate, and convinced in their faith.

His greasy, idle eyes were bent on the iconostasis. Familiar to him were the lengthy faces of the saints, the watchman Matvei, who puffed out his cheeks and blew out the candles, the tarnished candelabra, the threadbare carpet, the clerk Lopukhoff, who ran anxiously from the altar carrying the host to the sexton. All these things he had seen long ago, and again and again, as often as his five fingers. But one thing was unfamiliar. At the north door stood Father Grigori, still in priestly vestments, and angrily twitching his bushy eyebrows.

"What is he frowning at, God be with him?" thought the shopkeeper. "Yes, and he shakes his hand! And stamps his foot! Tell me what that means, please. What does it all mean, Heavenly Mother? Whom is he glaring at?"

Andrei Andreitch looked around, and saw that the church was already deserted. At the door thronged a dozen men, but their backs were turned to the altar.

"Come at once when you are called! Why do you stand there, looking like a statue?" came Father Grigori's angry voice. "I am calling *you!*"

The shopkeeper looked at Father Grigori's red, wrathful face, and for the first time realised that the frowning eyebrows and twitching fingers were directed at himself. He started, walked away from the choir, and resolutely, in his creaking goloshes, went up to the altar.

"Andrei Andreitch, was it you who handed this in during oblation, for the repose of Marya?" asked the priest, looking furiously at the shopkeeper's fat, perspiring face.

"Yes."

"So . . . and that means that you wrote it too? You?"

And Father Grigori wrathfully pushed a slip of paper under the shopkeeper's eyes. On this paper, given in by Andrei Andreitch during oblation, in a big, wandering hand, was written—

"Pray for the soul of God's slave, the Adulteress Marya."

"Exactly; I wrote it . . ." answered the shopkeeper.

"How dare you write such a thing?" whispered the priest slowly, and his hoarse whisper expressed indignation and horror.

The shopkeeper looked at him with dull amazement and doubt, and felt frightened; from the day of his birth, Father Grigori had never spoken so angrily to a member of the Verchniye Zaprudni "Intelligentsia." For a moment the two men faced each other in silence. The tradesman's surprise was so great that his fat face seemed to melt on all sides, as wet dough.

"How dare you?" repeated the priest.

"I don't understand," said Andrei Andreitch doubtfully.

"So you don't understand," whispered Father Grigori, receding in amazement, and flourishing his arms. "What have you got on your shoulders? A head, is it, or some other object? You hand a paper across the altar with a word which even in the street is regarded as improper! Why do you stick out your eyes? Is it possible you do not know the meaning of this word?"

"'This, I suppose, is all about the word 'adulteress,'" stammered the shopkeeper, reddening and blinking his eyes. "I see nothing wrong. Our Lord, in His mercy, this same thing . . . forgave an adulteress . . . prepared a place for her; yes, and the life of the blessed Mary of Egypt shows in what sense this word, excuse . . ."

The shopkeeper was about to adduce some other defence, but he lost the thread, and rubbed his lips with his cuff.

"So that's how you understand it!" The priest again flourished his hand impatiently. " You forget that our Lord forgave her—understand that—but you condemn her, you call her an improper name! And who is it? Your own daughter! Not merely in the sacred Scriptures, even in the profane, you will never read of such an act! I repeat to you, Andrei, don't try to be clever! Don't play the philosopher, brother! If God gave you a speculative head, and you don't know how to manage it, then better not speculate. . . . Don't try and be too clever—be silent!"

"Yes, but, you know, she . . . excuse my using the word, she was an actress," protested the shopkeeper.

"An actress! No matter what her career, it is your duty, once she's dead, to forget it, and not to write it on paper!"

"I understand . . ." consented the shopkeeper.

"You should be forced to do penance," growled the deacon from behind the altar, looking derisively at Andrei Andreitch's guilty face. "Then you'd soon drop your clever words. Your daughter was a well-known actress. Even in the newspapers they mentioned her death. . . . Philosopher!"

"I understand, of course . . . really," stammered the shopkeeper. "It was an unsuitable word, but I used it not in condemnation, Father Grigori; I wished to express myself scripturally . . . in short, to make you understand who it was you were to pray for. People always hand in some description, for instance: the infant John, the drowned woman Pelageya, the soldier Yegor, murdered Paul, and so on. . . . That is all I wanted."

"You are wrong, Andrei! God will forgive you, but take care the next time! And the chief thing is this; don't be too clever, and think like others. Abase yourself ten times and begone!"

"Yes," said the shopkeeper, rejoiced that the ordeal was over. His face again resumed its expression of

dignified self-importance. "Ten adorations! I understand. But now, *batiushka*, allow me to make a
request. Because I, after all, was her father . . .
you yourself know; in spite of everything she was my
daughter. I should like to ask you to say the mass
for her soul to-day. And I venture to ask you also,
father deacon!"

"That is right!" said Father Grigori, taking off
his surplice. "I praise you for that. I can approve
of it. . . . Now begone! We will come out at
once."

Andrei Andreitch walked heavily from the altar,
and, red-faced, with a solemn memorial-service expression, stood in the middle of the church. The watchman Matvei set before him a table with a crucifixion;
and after a brief delay the mass began.

The church was still. Audible only were the
censer's metallic ring and the droning voices. Near
Andrei Andreitch stood the watchman Matvei, the
midwife Makarievna, and her little son Mitka, with
the paralysed hand. No one else attended. The
clerk sang badly in an ugly, dull bass, but his words
were so mournful that the shopkeeper gradually lost
his pompous expression, and felt real grief. He
remembered his little Mashutka. . . . He remembered the day she was born, when he served as footman at Verchniye Zaprudni Hall; remembered how
in the rush of his footman's existence, he never noticed

that his little girl was growing up. Those long years during which she changed into a graceful girl, fair-haired, with eyes as big as copecks, sped away unobserved. He remembered that she was brought up, as the children of all the favoured servants, with the young ladies of the house; how the squire's family, merely from lack of other work, taught her to read, to write, and to dance; and how he, Andrei, took no part in her training. Only when at long intervals he met her at the gate, or on the landing, he would remember that she was his daughter and begin, as far as time allowed, to teach her her prayers and read from the Bible. Yes, and what fame he gained for knowledge of the rubric and the Holy Scriptures! And the little girl, however rigid and pompous her father's face, listened with delight. She yawned, it is true, as she repeated the prayers; but when, stammering and doing his best to speak magniloquently, he told her Bible stories she was all ears. And at Esau's lentils, the doom of Sodom, and the woes of little Joseph she turned pale, and opened wide her big blue eyes.

And then, when he retired from his post as footman, and with his savings opened a shop in the village, the family took Mashutka away to Moscow.

He remembered how three years before her death she came to him on a visit. She was already a young woman, graceful and well built, with the dress and

manners of a gentlewoman. And she spoke so
cleverly, as if out of a book, smoked cigarettes, and
slept till midday. Andrei Andreitch asked her what
was her business; and she, looking him straight in
the face, said boldly, "I am an actress!" And this
frank avowal seemed to the retired footman the height
of immodesty. Mashutka began to tell her father
of her stage triumphs and of her stage life; but
seeing her father's purple face, she stopped suddenly.
In silence, without exchanging a glance, they had
spent three weeks together until it was time for
Mashutka to go. Before leaving, she begged her
father to walk with her along the river bank. And,
shameful as it was to appear in daylight before
honest people with a daughter who was a vagrant
play-actress, he conceded her prayer.

"What glorious country you have!" she said
ecstatically as they walked. "What ravines, what
marshes! Heavens, how beautiful is my native
land!"

And she began to cry.

"Such things only take up space," thought Andrei
Andreitch, with a dull look at the ravines. He
understood nothing of his child's delight. "There
is as much use from them as milk from a goat!"

And she continued to cry, inhaling the air greedily,
as if she knew that her breaths were already num-
bered. . . .

Andrei Andreitch shook his head as a bitten horse, and to quench these painful memories, began to cross himself vigorously.

"Remember, Lord," he muttered, "thy dead slave, the Adulteress Marya, and forgive her all her sins!"

Again the improper word burst from his lips; but he did not notice it; what was set so deeply in his mind was not to be uprooted with a spade, much less by the admonitions of Father Grigori. Makarievna sighed, and whispered something, and paralysed Mitka seemed lost in thought.

". . . where there is neither sorrow, nor sickness, nor sighing!" droned the clerk, covering his face with his right hand. .

From the censer rose a pillar of blue smoke and swam in the broad, oblique sun-ray which cut the obscure emptiness of the church. And it seemed that with the smoke there floated in the sun-ray the soul of the dead girl. Eddies of smoke, like infants' curls, were swept upwards to the window; and the grief and affliction with which this poor soul was full seemed to pass away.

THE PRIVY COUNCILLOR

THE PRIVY COUNCILLOR

THE letter received at the beginning of April, 1870, by my widowed mother, Claudia Arkhipovna—my late father was an army lieutenant—came from her brother Ivan, a Privy Councillor in St. Petersburg. "Kidney disease," ran this letter, "compels me to spend all my summers abroad; but this year I have no ready money to spend on a visit to Marienbad, and it is very likely, dear sister, that I shall spend this summer with you at Kotchuefka. . . ."

When she had read the letter my mother turned pale and trembled. But her expression showed joy as well as grief. She wept, and she smiled. This combat of tears and laughter always reminded me of the hiss and sputter of a lighted candle when some one splashes it with water.

Having read the letter yet again, my mother summoned the whole household; and, her voice broken with emotion, explained that there had been four brothers Gundasoff—the first died a child, the second served in the army, and died also, the third—more shame to him—went on the stage, and the fourth . . .

"The fourth is at the top of the tree! . . ." sighed my mother. "My own brother, we grew up together, yet I fear to think of him! . . . He is a Privy Councillor, a general! How shall I meet my angel? What shall I say to him—I, an uneducated fool? For fifteen long years I haven't seen him once! Andriu-shenka!" My mother turned to me. "Rejoice, donkey! God has sent you your uncle for your future welfare!"

Her detailed history of the Gundasoffs heralded a household revolution hitherto witnessed only at Christmas. Only the river and the firmament were spared. Everything else within reach was scoured, scrubbed, and painted, and had the sky been smaller and nearer, had the river's course been slower, they too would have been rubbed with brick-bats and scoured with bast-ribbons. The walls, already whiter than snow, were whitewashed again; the floors already shone and sparkled, but they were re-washed thence-forward every day. The old cat Kutsi, so nicknamed after I had docked his tail with a sugar-knife, was exiled to the kitchen and handed over to Anisya, and Fedka was warned that "God would punish him" if the dogs came near the stairs. But the worst sufferings were reserved for the helpless carpets and arm-chairs. Never were they beaten so fiercely as on the eve of my uncle's advent. My pigeons, hearing the swish of the beaters' sticks, shuddered, and dis-appeared in the sky.

From Novostroefka came Spiridon, the only tailor within reach who could make clothes for gentlemen. As a man, Spiridon was sober, laborious, and capable, not devoid of imagination and a certain plastic sense; as a tailor he was beneath contempt. His lack of faith spoiled everything. From fear that his suits were not in the latest fashion, he took them to pieces as often as five times; he tramped miles into town to study the local fops; yet despite all his strivings, we were dressed in clothes which even a caricaturist would find pretentious and exaggerated. We spent our youth in such impossibly tight trousers and such short coats that the presence of girls always made us blush.

Spiridon spared no pains in measuring me. He measured me vertically and horizontally, as if he were about to hoop a barrel; he noted the details with a fat pencil; adorned his note-book with triangular signs; and, having done with me, seized hold of my tutor, Yegor Alekseievitch Pobiedimsky. My unforgotten tutor was then at the age when sprouting moustaches are a serious question and clothes are a problem of gravity, so you may imagine Spiridon's sacred terror as he began his measurements. He forced Pobiedimsky to throw back his head and spread his legs in an inverted V, to raise his arms on high, and again to lower them. Spiridon measured him again and again, marching round him as a love-sick dove round its mate; and then fell upon his knees, and doubled himself into a hook. My exhausted mother, tortured by the noise, red from prolonged ironing, watched the endless measuring, and said with gravity—

"Be careful, Spiridon, God will punish you if you spoil the cloth! If you make a failure you will never be happy again!"

Spiridon got red in the face and sweated, because he was firmly convinced already that he would make a failure. For making my suit he charged one rouble and twenty kopecks, for Pobiedimsky's two roubles, we supplying cloth, lining, and buttons; and this seems moderate enough when you learn that Novostroefka was ten versts away, and that the tailor came to try on at least four times. When during these operations we dragged on the tight trousers and skimpy jackets, still decked with basting threads, my mother frowned critically, and exclaimed—

"God knows what the fashions nowadays are like! They're painful even to look at! If it weren't for your uncle's visit, I'd ignore the fashion." And Spiridon, rejoiced that the fashions, not he, were guilty, shrugged his shoulders, and sighed as if to say—

"What are you to do? It's the spirit of the age."

The tension in which we waited our guest can be compared only with the emotion of spirit-rappers expecting a ghost. . . . My mother complained of headache, cried all day, and, as for me, I could neither eat nor sleep; and I neglected my lessons. Even in dreams I thirsted to see a general, that is, a man with epaulets, a braided collar up to his ears, and a naked sword—just such a general as hung above the drawing-room sofa, and glared from his threatening black eyes at all who dared to face him. Alone Pobiedimsky felt at ease. He showed neither fright nor elation; and sometimes, listening to mother's history of the Gundasoffs, said indifferently—

"Yes; it will be nice to have a new man to talk to."

All of us looked on my tutor as an exceptional man. He was young—about twenty—pimpled and untidy, and he had a small forehead and an extra-ordinarily long nose. His nose indeed was so long that to look intently at anything he had to turn his head aside, as a bird. Despite these defects, the household believed that the whole province could not produce an abler, more cultivated, more gallant man. He had been through all six classes of the gymnasium, but was expelled from a veterinary institute before he had been there half a year. As the cause of his expulsion was carefully concealed, those who liked him regarded him as a martyred, somewhat mysterious man. He spoke little, always on serious themes, ate meat during fasts, and looked with hauteur and con-tempt on the society around. This, indeed, did not hinder him accepting presents of clothes from my mother, or painting on my kites ugly faces with red teeth. My mother condemned his pride, but respected him for his brains.

Our guest arrived soon after his letter. At the beginning of May two carts laden with portmanteaux came from the railway station. So majestic were these portmanteaux that, unloading the carts, the drivers mechanically doffed their caps.

"I suppose," I reasoned, "all these are full of uniforms and powder." My conception of a general was indissolubly bound with cannons and powder.

On the morning of the 10th of May my nurse informed me in a whisper that uncle had come. I dressed quickly, washed myself recklessly, and without saying my prayers, rushed out of the room. In the hall I nearly collided with a tall, stout gentleman with fashionably trimmed whiskers and a smart over-coat. Frozen with sacred terror, and remembering the ceremony of greeting taught by my mother, I shuffled my feet, bowed deeply, and bent over his hand. But the gentleman refused to allow me to kiss his hand, and added that he was not my uncle, but only his servant, Piotr. The sight of this Piotr, who was better dressed than I or Pobiedimsky, caused me intense surprise, which survives indeed to this day, for I cannot understand how such solid, representative men with clever, severe faces, can serve as valets. Piotr told me that my uncle was in the garden with my mother. I rushed into the garden.

Nature, being unconscious both of the Gundasoff pedigree and of uncle's official rank, was much freer and more at ease than I. The tumult in the garden reminded me of a fair. Innumerable starlings clove the air, hopped on the paths, and with noise and cries hunted the May-flies. Sparrows rustled in the lilac trees, whose delicate, perfumed blooms stretched out at my face. On all sides orioles sang, hoopoes and hawks flew. On any other occasion I should have hunted the dragon-flies or thrown stones at the crow on the hayrick close by the aspen, and bent its blunt nose, but now I was in no mood for such pranks. My heart palpitated; I felt a chill in my stomach; I prepared to see an epauletted hero with a naked sword and terrible menacing eyes.

Imagine my disappointment! By the side of my mother walked a little, slender fop in white jacket and trousers and white forage cap. With hands in pockets, head thrown back—sometimes almost running in front—he had the air of a mere youth. His figure showed extreme briskness and life, and treacherous age was betrayed only behind by a patch of silver-grey hair under the edge of his cap. Instead of a general's solidity and stiffness, there was a boyish nimbleness; instead of a collar stiff to the ears, an ordinary blue necktie. My mother and my uncle walked down the path and talked. I followed them, waiting patiently till one or the other should turn.

" What a ravishing little home you have, Claudia ! "
said my uncle. " How sweet! How charming! Had
I known that you lived in such a paradise, nothing
would have induced me to spend my summers abroad
in past years."

My uncle bent in two and smelt a tulip. Everything that met his eyes inspired, it seemed, interest
and delight; it was as if for the first time in life he
had seen a garden and a sunny day. The strange
man walked as if on springs and chattered without
cease, so that my mother never spoke a word. At
a corner of the path from behind an elder-bush
suddenly appeared Pobiedimsky. His appearance was
unexpected. My uncle started and took a step to the
rear. My tutor wore his best cloak, in which, viewed
from behind, he closely resembled a windmill. His
air was solemn and dignified. Pressing, as a Spaniard,
his hat to his breast, he took one step towards uncle
and bowed, as marquises bow in melodramas—forward
and a little on one side.

" I have the honour to introduce myself to your
Excellency," he said loudly. " I am a pedagogue,
the tutor of your nephew, an ex-veterinary student,
and a noble, Pobiedimsky ! "

My tutor's polished manners pleased my mother
intensely. She smiled and waited expectantly, hoping
that Pobiedimsky would say something brilliant. But
my tutor, who expected that his impressive greeting

would be received equally impressively—that is, that
my uncle, like a true general, would answer
"H-m-m-m!" and extend two of his fingers—lost
his self-possession when my uncle smiled at him
genially and warmly pressed his hand. He muttered
incoherently, coughed, and turned aside.

"He's too delightful for words," said my uncle,
smiling. "Just look at him! He's put on his best
manners, and finds himself a very clever man! I like
it, I swear to God! What youthful aplomb, what
realism in this droll magniloquence! And who is
this little boy?" he asked, turning suddenly and
catching sight of me.

"That is my Andriushenka," said my mother,
blushing. "My only treasure!"

I shuffled my feet on the gravel and bowed low.

"And a fine little fellow . . . a first-rate boy,"
muttered my uncle, taking his hand from his lips
and stroking my head. "So you're called Andriushenka. Indeed. . . . A fine little boy! I swear to
God! . . . You learn your lessons?"

. My mother, boasting and exaggerating, described
my progress in learning and manners, and I walked
beside my uncle, and, remembering the protocol,
never ceased to bow to the ground. My mother
hinted that with such remarkable talents I should
enter the Cadets' Corpus at the State's expense; and
I, still observing the protocol, was about to weep

and beg my kinsman's protection, when suddenly my
uncle started and opened his arms with a look of
intense surprise.

"Lord in heaven, what is that?" he asked.

Down the path came Tatiana Ivanovna, wife of
Feodor Petrovitch, our steward. She was carrying a
white, well-starched petticoat, and a long ironing
board. When passing she looked timidly at the guest
through her long eyelashes, and blushed.

"Still more miracles!" cried my uncle, through
his teeth, looking genially after her. "One can't
walk a yard with you, sister, without a fresh surprise. . . . I swear to God!"

"That is our local beauty," said my mother. "She
was courted for Feodor in town, a hundred versts
from this."

Few would have found Tatiana Ivanovna beautiful.
She was a little plump woman of about twenty, black-
browed, and always rosy and pleasing. But neither
face nor figure contained one striking trait, one bold
stroke to catch the eye; it seemed as if Nature,
creating her, had lost inspiration and confidence.
Tatiana Ivanovna was timid, confused, and well-man-
nered; she walked quietly and smoothly, spoke little,
and seldom smiled; her whole life was as flat and event-
less as her face and her smoothly dressed hair. My uncle
looked after her and smiled; and my mother looked
earnestly at her smiling face, and became serious.

"And you, brother . . . so you never married!"
She sighed.

"Never!"

"Why?" asked my mother softly.

"It's hard to explain. Somehow it worked out that way. When young I worked hard, and thought little of such things; and when I began to feel the desire to live, I suddenly remembered that I was over fifty. . . . I never, somehow, managed to get married. But that is a tiresome subject."

My mother and my uncle both sighed, and went on. I remained behind and sought my tutor to exchange impressions. Pobiedimsky stood in the middle of the yard and looked solemnly at the sky.

"You can see that he is a cultivated man," he said. "I hope we shall get on with him."

An hour later my mother returned to us.

"What a pity, my dears!" she began. "My brother has brought a servant; and a servant, God love him, whom I can't put in the kitchen, or the hall. He must have a room to himself. I don't know how to manage. The two of you must remove into the wing with Feodor, and give up your room to the valet."

We consented readily. There was more freedom in the wing than under my mother's eyes.

"But that's not the worst!" continued my mother. "Your uncle says he will dine late, at seven o'clock, as at St. Petersburg. I'll go out of my mind! At seven the dinner will be cooked to death. In spite of their big brains, men never understand house-keeping. We must have two dinners. You, my dears, will dine early as before; I, old woman, will wait till seven for my brother's sake."

My mother sighed deeply, advised me to please my uncle, whom God had sent for my welfare, and ran into the kitchen. Pobiedimsky and I migrated to the wing, where we made ourselves cosy in a room with two doors, between the hall and the steward's bedroom.

My uncle's arrival and our migration made little difference in our lives. Contrary to expectation, things remained as of old, drowsy and monotonous. Pobiedimsky, who read no books and had no interests in life, sat hours on his bed, moved his long nose, and thought. Occasionally he rose, tried on his new suit, and again sat, silent and thoughtful. The flies alone worried him, and he slapped them ruthlessly. After dinner when he usually "rested," his snores caused agony to the whole household. As for me, morning to night I ran wild about the garden or sat in the wing and glued my kites. For the first few weeks we seldom even saw my uncle. All day long, ignoring the flies and the heat, he sat in his room and worked. His capacity for sitting still at his desk smacked of magic; and for us, idlers with no regular occupations, his industry was a miracle. Rising at nine o'clock, he sat at once at his desk, and worked steadily till dinner. After dinner he resumed his work, and continued it till late at night. Sometimes I peered through the keyhole; and always saw the same scene: my uncle sat at his desk and worked; and his work seemed always the same: with one hand he wrote, with the other he turned over the pages of a book; and—what seemed strangest to me—his body moved without cease; he swung his leg as a pendulum, whistled and nodded his head in time. His face expressed levity and abstraction, as if he were playing noughts and crosses. He always wore the same short, smart jacket and the same well-tied necktie, and even through the keyhole I could smell his delicate, feminine perfumes. He left his room only to dine, and then ate hardly anything.

"I can't understand your uncle," complained my mother. "Every day for him alone we kill a turkey and pigeons, and I make compotes with my own hands; but all he touches is a plate of bouillon and a piece of bread, and then goes back to his desk. He'll die of starvation. When I argue with him about it he only smiles and jokes. No, he doesn't like our food!"

Evening was pleasanter than day. At sunset when long shadows lay across the road, Tatiana Ivanovna, Pobiedimsky, and I sat on the steps of the wing. Till dark, we kept silence—indeed, what was there fresh to say?—the one new theme, my uncle's visit,

had been worn threadbare. Pobiedimsky kept his
eyes on Tatiana Ivanovna's face and sighed unceasingly.
At that time I misinterpreted these sighs, and missed
their real meaning; afterwards they explained much.

When the long shadows merged in the general
gloom, Feodor, the steward, returned from shooting
or from the farm. Feodor always impressed me as
a savage, terrible person. The son of a Russianised
gipsy, swarthy, with big black eyes and a curly ill-
kept beard, he was nicknamed "devilkin" by the
Kotchuefka peasants. His ways were as gipsy as his
face. He was restless at home; and whole days
wandered about, shooting game, or simply walking
across country. Morose, bilious, and taciturn, he
feared no one and respected no authority. To my
mother he was openly rude, he addressed me as
"thou," and held my tutor's learning in contempt.
Looking on him as a delicate, excitable man, we
forgave him all this; and my mother liked him,
because, notwithstanding his gipsy ways, he was
ideally honest and hard - working. He loved his
Tatiana Ivanovna with a gipsy's love, but his affection
expressed itself darkly, as if it caused him pain.
Indeed, in our presence he showed no regard for his
wife, but stared at her steadily and viciously and
contorted his mouth.

On returning from the farm he set down his gun
noisily and viciously in the wing, came out to us on

the stairs, and sat beside his wife. After a minute's rest, he put a few questions about housekeeping, and relapsed into silence.

"Let us have a song."

My tutor played the guitar, and, in the thick, bass voice of a church clerk, sang "Among the level valleys." All joined in. The tutor sang bass, Feodor in a hardly audible tenor, and I soprano, in one voice with Tatiana Ivanovna.

When the sky was covered with stars and the frogs ceased croaking, supper was brought from the kitchen. We went indoors and ate. My tutor and the gipsy ate greedily and so noisily that it was hard to judge whether they were eating bones or merely crunching their jaws. Tatiana Ivanovna and I barely finished our portions. After supper the wing sank to deep sleep.

Once—it was at the end of May—we sat on the steps and waited for supper, when a shadow fell across us, and suddenly as if sprung out of the ground appeared Gundasoff. For a second he looked at us steadfastly, then waved his hands, and smiled a merry smile.

"An idyll!" he exclaimed. "They sing; they dream of the moon! It's irresistible, I swear to God! May I sit with you and dream?"

We exchanged looks, but said nothing. My uncle seated himself on the lowest step, yawned, and looked at the sky. At first silence reigned; and it was Pobiedimsky, long watching for an opportunity to speak with some one new, who broke it. For such intellectual conversation Pobiedimsky had only one theme—epizooty. As a man who has been in a crowd a thousand strong sometimes remembers one face in particular, so Pobiedimsky, of all he had read at the Institute during his six months' studies, retained only one phrase:

"Epizooty is the cause of untold loss to agriculture. In combating it the public must itself walk hand in hand with the authorities."

Before saying this to Gundasoff, my tutor thrice cleared his throat, and pulled his cloak nervously around him. When he had heard about epizooty my uncle looked earnestly at Pobiedimsky, and emitted a queer sound through his nose.

"I swear to God! . . ." he stammered, looking at us as if we were manikins. "This is indeed the real life. . . . This is what life should really be. And you, why are you so silent, Pelageya Ivanovna?" he said, turning to Tatiana Ivanovna, who reddened and coughed.

"Talk, ladies and gentlemen; sing . . . play! Lose no time! Time, the rascal, is flying . . . he won't wait. I swear to God—before you've had time to turn your head, old age is on you. . . . It's too late then to live! Isn't that so, Pelageya Ivanovna? On no account sit still and keep silence. . . ."

Supper was brought in from the kitchen. Uncle

followed us into the wing, and, for company's sake, ate five curd-fritters and a duck's wing. As he ate he looked at us. We seemed to inspire nothing but rapture and emotion. The worst nonsense of my tutor, every act of Tatiana Ivanovna, he found charming and entrancing. When after supper Tatiana Ivanovna sat quietly in a corner and knitted away, he kept his eyes on her fingers and chattered without cease.

"You, my friends, hurry up; make haste to live! God forbid that you should sacrifice to-day for to-morrow! The present is yours; it brings youth, health, ardour—the future is a mirage, smoke! As soon as you reach the age of twenty you must begin to live!"

Tatiana Ivanovna dropped a knitting-needle. My uncle hopped from his seat, recovered and restored it, with a bow which told me for the first time that there were men in the world more gallant than Pobiedimsky.

"Yes," continued my uncle. "Love, marry! . . . Play the fool! Follies are much more vital and sane than labours such as mine, saner far than our efforts to lead a rational life. . . ."

My uncle spoke much, in fact at such length that we soon grew tired, and I sat aside on a box, listened, and dreamed. I was offended because he never once turned his attention on me. He stayed in the wing

until two in the morning, when I, no longer able
to resist my drowsiness, slept soundly.

From that day on, my uncle came to the wing
every night. He sang with us, supped with us, and
stayed till two in the morning, chattering incessantly
of one and the same subject. His night work was
forgotten, and at the end of June, by which time
he had learnt to eat my mother's turkeys and
compotes, his daily occupation was also neglected.
He tore himself from his desk, and rushed, so to
speak, into "life." By day he marched about the
garden, whistled, and hindered the workmen, forcing
them to tell him stories. When Tatiana Ivanovna
came within sight, he ran up to her, and if she
carried a load, offered to help her, causing her endless confusion.

The longer summer lasted the more frivolous,
lively, and abstracted grew my uncle. Pobiedimsky
was quickly disillusioned.

"As a man—one-sided," was his verdict. "No
one would believe that he stands on the high steps
of the official hierarchy. He doesn't even speak well.
After every word he adds 'I swear to God!' No,
I don't like him."

From the night of my uncle's first visit to the
wing, Feodor and my tutor changed noticeably.
Feodor gave up shooting, returned early from his
work, and his taciturnity increased; and, when my

uncle was present, looked still more viciously at his wife. Pobiedimsky ceased to speak about epizootic diseases, frowned, and sometimes smiled ironically.

"Here comes our mouse-foal!" he growled once, as uncle approached the wing.

Searching for an explanation, I concluded that both had taken offence. My uncle confused their names, and to the day of his departure had not learnt which was my tutor and which Tatiana Ivanovna's husband. As for Tatiana Ivanovna, he called her indiscriminately "Nastasya," "Pelageya," and "Yevdokia." In his emotion and delight he treated all four of us as young children. All of which, of course, might easily be taken as offensive by young people. But the cause of the change of manner lay not in this, but, as I soon understood, in subtler shades of feeling.

I remember one evening I sat on a box and fought my desire to sleep. My eyelids drooped, my body, fatigued with a day's hard exercise, fell on one side. It was nearly midnight. Tatiana Ivanovna, rosy and meek, as always, sat at a little table and mended her husband's underclothes. From one corner glared Feodor, grim and morose; in another sat Pobiedimsky, hidden behind his high collar, and angrily snoring. My uncle, lost in thought, walked from corner to corner. No one spoke, the only sound was the rustling of the cloth in Tatiana's hands. My uncle suddenly stopped in front of Tatiana Ivanovna, and said—

H

"There you are; all so young, so good, living so restfully in this refuge that I envy you! I have got so used to this life that my heart sinks when I think I must leave you. . . . Believe in me; I am sincere."

Slumber closed my eyes, and I lost consciousness. I was awakened by a noise, and saw that my uncle still stood before Tatiana Ivanovna, and looked at her with rapture. His cheeks burned.

" My life is past," he said. " I have never lived. Your young face reminds me of my vanished youth. I should rejoice to sit here and look at you till the day of my death! With what joy could I take you back with me to St. Petersburg!"

"What is the meaning of this?" asked Feodor hoarsely.

" I should set you down on my desk under a glass case, and admire you, and show you to my friends. Pelageya Ivanovna, such as you we have none! We have wealth, distinction, sometimes beauty! But never this living sincerity . . . this healthy restfulness."

My uncle sat down before Tatiana Ivanovna and took her by the hand.

" So you don't want to come to St. Petersburg," he continued caressingly. " In that case give me here your little handy! Adorable little handy! You won't give it? Well, miser, at least let me give it a kiss! . . ."

A chair moved noisily. Feodor leaped up, and with measured, heavy footsteps, went up to his wife. His face was pale grey, and trembled. With his whole force he banged his fist on the table, and said in a hoarse voice—

"I will not tolerate this!"

And at the same moment Pobiedimsky jumped from his chair. As pale as Feodor and looking equally vicious, he strode up to Tatiana Ivanovna, and banged his fist on the table.

"I will not . . . tolerate this!" he exclaimed.

"I don't understand. What is the matter?" asked my uncle.

"I will not tolerate this!" repeated Feodor. And again he banged his fist noisily on the table.

My uncle rose from his seat and blinked timidly. He tried to say something, but astonishment and fright prevented him uttering a word; and, leaving his hat behind, he tottered with old-man's steps out of the wing. When a little later my terrified mother ran into the wing, Feodor and Pobiedimsky, like a pair of blacksmiths, were banging their fists on the table and roaring, "I will not tolerate this!"

"What on earth has happened?" asked my mother. "Why have you insulted my brother? What is the matter?"

But seeing Tatiana Ivanovna's pale, frightened face and the glare of her raging husband, my mother quickly guessed what was the matter. She sighed and shook her head.

"Don't bang the table again! Feodor, stop! And why are you banging the table, Yegor Alexeievitch? What has this to do with you?"

Pobiedimsky staggered back in confusion. Feodor gave him a piercing glance, then looked at his wife, and walked up the room. But the moment my mother left I witnessed what at first I thought must be a dream. I saw Feodor seizing my tutor, lifting him high in the air, and flinging him violently against the door.

When I awoke next morning my tutor's bed was empty. My nurse whispered that he had been taken to hospital that morning and that his arm was broken. Saddened by this news, and with my mind full of the scandal of the night before, I went into the yard. The weather was dull. The sky was veiled with clouds, and a strong wind blew, carrying before it dust, papers, and feathers. I foresaw rain. The faces of men and animals expressed tedium. When I returned to the house I was ordered to walk on tip-toes as my mother had a bad headache and was lying down. What was to be done? I went out to the gate, sat on a bench, and tried to pierce to the meaning of all that I had seen and heard. From our gates ran a road, which, passing the smithy and a pond which never dried up, converged with the post-road. I looked at the telegraph posts and the clouds of dust around them, and at the sleepy birds perched on the trees, and felt so oppressed by tedium that I began to cry.

Down the post-road drove a dusty double droschky full of townspeople, probably on a pilgrimage. When the droschky disappeared a light victoria drawn by a pair came in sight. In this victoria, holding the coachman's belt, stood the police commissary, Akim Nikititch. To my amazement, the victoria turned up our road, and flew past me to the gate. While I was seeking the reason of the commissary's visit a troika came in sight. In the troika stood the inspector of police, and showed the coachman our gate.

"What does it all mean?" I asked myself, looking at the dust-covered inspector. Pobiedimsky, I guessed, had complained, and the police had come to arrest and carry off Feodor.

But I solved the riddle wrongly. The commissary and inspector were only heralds of another, for five minutes later yet another carriage arrived. It flashed so quickly by me that I could see only that the occupant had a red beard.

Lost in astonishment and foreboding evil, I ran into the house. I met my mother in the hall. Her face was white, and she looked with terror at the door from which came the voices of men. The visitors had caught her unawares when her headache was at its worst.

"What is it, mother?" I asked.

" Sister," came my uncle's voice. "Let the governor have something to eat."

"It's easy enough to say," whispered my mother. "I have no time to get anything done. I am disgraced in my old age!"

With her hands to her head, my mother flew into the kitchen. The governor's unexpected arrival turned the whole house upside down. A merciless massacre began. Ten chickens, five turkeys, eight ducks were slaughtered at once; and through carelessness the servants decapitated an old gander, the ancestor of our flock, and the beloved of my mother. To prepare some miserable sauce perished a pair of my pigeons, which were as dear to me as the gander to my mother. It was long before I forgave the governor their death.

That evening, when the governor, his son, and his suite, having dined to repletion, took their seats in their carriages and drove away, I went into the house to survey the remains of the feast. In the drawing-room were my uncle and my mother. My uncle walked excitedly up and down the room and shrugged his shoulders. My mother, exhausted and haggard, lay on a sofa, and followed my uncle's movements with staring eyes.

"Forgive me, sister, but this is impossible!" groaned my uncle, with a frown. "I introduced the governor to you, and you didn't even shake hands

with him. . . . You made the poor man uncomfortable! Such things are impossible. I swear to God!
. . . And then this dinner? For instance, what on
earth was that fourth course?"

"It was duck with sweet sauce," answered my
mother softly.

"Duck! . . . Forgive me, sister, but . . . I
have got heartburn . . . I am unwell!"

My uncle made a sour and lachrymose grimace,
and continued—

"The devil brought us this governor! A lot I
wanted his visit! . . . Heartburn! I can't sleep and
I can't work. . . . I am altogether out of sorts.
. . . I cannot understand how you exist without
work . . . in this tiresome place! And I have got
a pain beginning in the lower part of my chest!"

My uncle frowned, and walked still more quickly.

"Brother," asked my mother timidly, "how much
would it cost you to go abroad?"

"At least three thousand," answered my uncle
tearfully. "I should have gone, but where can I get
the money? I have not a kopeck. . . . Heartburn!"

My uncle stopped, looked with disgust at the big,
dull window, and resumed his walk. My mother
looked earnestly at the ikon, broke out into tears,
and said with an effort—

"I will let you have the three thousand, brother!"

Three days afterwards the majestic portmanteaux were sent to the railway station, and away after them whirled the Privy Councillor. Taking leave of my mother, he wept, and pressed his lips to her hand; but once seated in the carriage his face grew radiant with infantile joy. Smiling, complacent, he seated himself comfortably, waved his hand to my weeping mother, and suddenly turned his eyes on me. On his face appeared a look of extreme astonishment.

"And who is this little boy?" he asked.

My mother, who had assured me that God had sent my uncle for my welfare, was struck dumb by the question. But it had no import for me. I looked at my uncle's smiling face and suddenly felt for him sincere compassion. Unable to contain my feelings, I climbed on the carriage, and warmly embraced my weak and frivolous relative. I looked into his eyes, and wishing to say something pleasant, asked—

"Uncle, did you ever fight in a war?"

"*Akh*, darling boy!" smiled my uncle, kissing me tenderly. "Dear little boy! I swear to God. All this is so natural, so true to life. I swear to God!"

The carriage started. I gazed after it earnestly, and long continued to hear the farewell exclamation, "I swear to God!"

THE RUNAWAY

THE RUNAWAY

IT was an endless affair. Pashka and his mother, drenched with rain, tramped mile after mile, first across stubble fields, then by soft woodland paths where yellow leaves stuck to his boots, and on and on till daybreak. After that he stood two hours in a dark entrance-hall, and waited for the doors to open. In the hall, of course, it was warmer and drier than outside; but even there the piercing wind carried the raindrops in. And as the hall slowly filled with patients, Pashka, wedging his way through the crowd, pressed his face against a sheepskin coat which smelt strongly of salted fish, and slumbered.

At last the bolt slipped, the door opened, and Pashka and his mother found themselves in the waiting-room. Yet another long delay! The patients sat on benches; no one stirred; no one opened his mouth. Pashka stared at the crowd, and likewise held his tongue, though he witnessed many ludicrous, inexplicable things. But once when a boy hopped into the room on one leg, he nudged his mother's side, grinned in his sleeve, and exclaimed—

"Look, mother—a sparrow!"

"Don't talk, child, don't talk!"

At a little window appeared the *feldscher's* sleepy face. "Come and give your names."

The waiting patients, among them the funny, hopping boy, crowded round the window. Of each the *feldscher* asked name and patronymic, age, village, dates of illness, and other questions. From his mother's answer, Pashka learnt that his name was Pavl Galaktionoff, that he was seven years old, and that he had been ill since Easter.

When the names were entered there was another short delay; and then through the waiting-room walked the doctor, in white apron, with a towel on his shoulder. As he passed the hopping boy, he shrugged his shoulders, and said in a sing-song voice—

"You're a donkey! Now aren't you a donkey? I told you Monday, and you come on Friday! Don't worry yourself so far as I'm concerned, but if you're not careful, fool, you'll lose your leg!"

The hopping boy blinked, grimaced piteously as if asking for alms, and began—

"Ivan Nikolaitch, be so kind . . ."

"None of your Ivan Nikolaitch!" said the doctor teasingly. "I told you Monday—you should obey! You're a donkey, that's all."

The reception began. The doctor sat in his room,

and called for the patients in turn. Now and then from the room came shrill exclamations, the sobs of children, and the doctor's angry exclamations—

"Don't howl. I won't murder you! Sit quiet!"

At last came Pashka's turn. "Pavl Galaktionoff!" cried the doctor. Pashka's mother at first seemed dazed, as if the summons were unexpected; but she recovered herself, took Pashka's hand, and led him into the doctor's room. The doctor sat on a table, and tapped mechanically with a mallet a thick book.

"What is the matter?" he asked, without looking at his visitors.

"My boy has a boil, *batiushka*, on his elbow," answered Pashka's mother; and her expression implied that she herself was suffering from Pashka's boil.

"Take off his clothes!"

Pashka, panting, untied his neckkerchief, rubbed his nose on his sleeve, and began to unbutton his coat.

"Woman! have you come to pay me a visit?" said the doctor irritably. "Why don't you hurry? Are you the only one waiting?"

Pashka hurriedly threw his coat on the floor, and, with his mother's help, took off his shirt. The doctor looked at him absent-mindedly, and slapped him on the bare stomach.

"Serious, brother Pashka," he exclaimed. "You

have outgrown your corporation!" When he had
said this, he sighed, and added, "Show me your
elbow!"

Pashka took fright at a bowl of blood-tinged
water, looked at the doctor's apron, and began to
cry.

"For shame!" said the doctor mockingly. "He's
big enough to get married, yet he begins to howl.
For shame!"

Pashka tried to stop his tears. He looked at his
mother, and his expression said, "Don't tell them
at home that I cried at the hospital."

The doctor examined the elbow, pinched it, sighed,
smacked his lips, and again felt the elbow.

"You ought to be whipped, woman!" he said.
"Why didn't you bring him sooner? His arm is
nearly gone! Look at him, idiot, can't you see that
the joint is diseased?"

"It is you who know best, *batiushka!*" said
Pashka's mother.

"*Batiushka!* the lad's arm is rotting off, and you
with your *batiushka!* What sort of a workman will
he make without arms? You'll have to nurse him
all his life! If you've got a pimple on your nose
you run off here for treatment, but you let your own
child rot for six months! You people are all the
same!"

He lighted a cigarette. While it burned away he

scolded Pashka's mother, hummed a tune, shook his head rhythmically, and thought something out. Naked Pashka stood before him, listened to the tune, and watched the smoke. When the cigarette went out the doctor started, and said in a low voice—

"Listen, woman! Ointments and mixtures are no use in this case; you must leave him here."

"If it must be so, *batiushka*, so be it."

"We must have an operation. . . . And you, Pashka, you must stay," said the doctor, patting his shoulder. "We will let mother go, but you, brother, you will stay with me. It is not bad here, brother! I have raspberry bushes. You and I, Pashka, as soon as we get better, will go and catch thrushes, and I will show you a fox. We shall pay visits together. Eh? Will you stay? And mother will come for you to-morrow."

Pashka looked questioningly at his mother.

"You must stay, child," she said.

"Of course he'll stay," said the doctor merrily. "There is nothing to argue about! I'll show him a live fox. We'll drive to the fair and buy sugar-candy. Marya Denisovna, take him upstairs!"

The doctor was certainly a merry, talkative man; and Pashka was attracted, all the more because he had never been at a fair, and wanted to see a live fox. But his mother? He thought the problem out, and decided to ask the doctor to let his mother remain with him; but before he could open his mouth the nurse was leading him upstairs. With mouth wide open, he looked around. The stairs, the floors, the door-posts, all were painted a beautiful yellow; and everywhere there was a tempting smell of fast-butter. Everywhere hung lamps, everywhere lay carpets; and brass water-taps projected from every wall. But most of all Pashka was pleased by his bed with its grey, shaggy counterpane. He felt the pillows and the counterpane, and came to the conclusion that the doctor had a very nice house.

It was a little ward with only three cots. The first was vacant, the second Pashka's; and on the third sat a very old man with sour eyes, who coughed without cease, and spat into a bowl. From his bed Pashka could see through the open door part of another ward with two beds; on one lay a thin, very pallid man with a caoutchouc bladder on his head. A peasant, arms apart, with bandaged head, looking very like an old woman, sat on the other.

Having set Pashka on his bed, the nurse left him. She returned immediately with an armful of clothes. "These are for you," she said to him. "Put them on." Pashka took off his old clothes, and, not without pleasure, arrayed himself in his new garments. After donning a shirt, a pair of trousers, and a grey dressing-gown, he looked at himself complacently, and thought how he would like to walk down the village

street in his new clothes. Imagination painted his
mother sending him to the kitchen garden by the
river, to pluck cabbage leaves for the pig, while the
village boys and girls stood round him and gaped
enviously at his dressing-gown.

When next the nurse returned she brought two
tin bowls, two spoons, and two slices of bread. She
gave one bowl to the old man, and the other to
Pashka. "Eat!" she said.

When Pashka examined the bowl he found it full
of greasy soup with a piece of meat at the bottom;
and again he reasoned that the doctor lived very comfortably, and was not half as angry as he seemed.
He dallied over the soup, licked the spoon after each
mouthful, and when nothing remained but the meat,
cast a sidelong glance at the old man, and felt envy.
With a sigh, he began the meat, trying to make it
last as long as possible. But his efforts were in vain ;
the meat vanished speedily. There remained only
the bread. Bread without condiment is tasteless food,
but there was no remedy ; after weighing the problem,
he ate the bread also. And just as he had finished
it the nurse arrived with two more bowls. This time
the bowls contained roast beef and potatoes.

"Where is your bread?" she asked. Pashka did
not answer, but distended his cheeks and puffed out
the air.

"You've gobbled it up?" said the nurse reproach-

I

fully. "What will you eat your meat with?" She
left him, and returned with more bread. Never in
his life had Pashka eaten roast beef, and, trying it
now, he found it very tasty. But it disappeared in a
few seconds; and again only the bread was left, a
bigger slice than the first. The old man, having
finished his dinner, hid his bread in a drawer; and
Pashka resolved to do the same, but after a moment's
hesitation, he ate it up.

After dinner he set out to explore. In the next
ward he found four men, in addition to those he had
seen from his bed. Only one drew his attention.
This was a tall, skeleton peasant, morose and hairy-
faced, who sat on his bed, shook his head incessantly,
and waved his arms pendulum-wise. Pashka could not
tear his eyes away. At first the peasant's measured
pendulum movements seemed droll, and made for the
amusement of onlookers; but when Pashka looked at
the peasant's face, he understood that this meant
intolerable pain, and he felt sorry. In the third ward
were two men with dark-red faces—red as if plastered
with clay. They sat up motionless in bed, and, with
their strange faces and nearly hidden features, resembled heathen gods.

"Auntie, why are they like that?" he asked the
nurse.

"They are small-pox patients, laddie."

When Pashka returned to his own room he sat on

his bed, and waited for the doctor to come and catch thrushes or drive to the fair. But the doctor tarried. At the door of the next ward the *feldscher* stood for a moment. He bent over the patient with the ice-bag, and cried—

"Mikhailo!"

But sleeping Mikhailo did not hear. The *feldscher* waved his hand, and went away. While waiting for the doctor, Pashka looked at his neighbour. The old man continued to cough, and spit into the bowl, and his cough was drawn-out and wheezy. But one thing pleased Pashka intensely. When the old man, having coughed, inhaled a breath, something whistled in his chest, and sang in different notes.

"Grandfather, what is that whistling in your inside?" asked Pashka.

The old man did not answer. Pashka waited a minute, and began again.

"Grandfather, where is the fox?"

"What fox?"

"The live one."

"Where should it be? In the wood, of course."

The hours slipped by, but no doctor came. At last the nurse brought Pashka's tea, and scolded him for having eaten the bread; the *feldscher* returned and tried to waken Mikhailo; the lamps were lighted; but still no doctor. It was already too late to drive to the fair or catch thrushes. Pashka stretched himself on

his bed and began to think.   He thought of the
doctor's promised sugar-candy, of his mother's face
and voice, of the darkness in the cabin at home, of
querulous Yegorovna.   And he suddenly felt tedium
and grief.   But remembering that his mother would
come in the morning, he smiled, and fell asleep.

He was awakened by a noise.   Men walked in the
adjoining ward and spoke in whispers.   The dim gleam
of nightlights and lamps showed three figures moving
near Mikhailo's bed.

"Shall we take him on the mattress, or as he is?"
asked one.

"As he is.   There's no room for the mattress. *Akh*,
he's dead at a bad hour, heaven rest his soul!"

Then—one of the figures taking Mikhailo's shoulders,
another his feet—they lifted him, and the folds of his
dressing-gown hung limply in the air.   The third—
it was the woman-like peasant—crossed himself; and
all three, shuffling their feet, tripping in the folds of
the dressing-gown, went out of the ward.

The sleeping man's chest whistled, and sang in different notes.   Pashka heard it, looked in fright at the
black windows, and jumped out of bed in panic.

"Mother!" he screamed.

And, without awaiting an answer, he rushed into the
adjoining ward.   The lamps and nightlights barely
banished the gloom; the patients, agitated by Mikhailo's death, were sitting up in their beds.   Grim,

dishevelled, haunted by shades, they looked like giants;
they seemed to increase in size; and far away in a dark
corner sat a peasant nodding his head and swinging
his pendulous hands. Without seeing the door, Pashka
tore through the small-pox ward into the corridor,
thence into an endless chamber full of long-haired
monsters with ancient faces. He flew through the
women's ward, again reached the corridor, recognised
the balustrade, and rushed downstairs. And there,
finding himself in the waiting-room where he had sat
that morning, he looked wildly for the door.

The latch rattled, a cold wind blew, and Pashka,
stumbling, sped into the yard, in his head a single
thought: to flee, to flee! He did not know the road,
but felt that it was enough to run without cease and
that he would soon be at home with his mother. The
moon shone through the clouds of an overcast sky.
Pashka ran straight ahead, dashed round a shed into
the shrubbery, stood a second in doubt, then rushed
back to the hospital and ran around it. But there
he stopped in indecision, for suddenly before his eyes
rose the white crosses of a graveyard.

"Mother!" he screamed, and turned back again.

And at last, as he dashed past the black, menacing
building, he saw a lighted window.

In the darkness, the bright red patch breathed
terror. But Pashka, mad with panic, unknowing
whither to flee, turned towards it with relief. Beside

the window were steps and a hall door with a white
notice-board. Pashka rushed up the steps, and looked
through the window. A sharp, breathless joy suddenly
seized him. For there in the window at a table sat
the merry, talkative doctor with a book in his hands.
Pashka laughed with joy; he tried to cry out; but
some irresistible force suppressed his breath, and struck
him on the legs, and he staggered and fell senseless on
the steps.

When he came to himself it was quite light; and
the sing-song voice that had promised the fair, the
thrushes, and the live fox whispered in his ear—

"You're a donkey, Pashka! Now aren't you a
donkey? You ought to be whipped. . . ."

THE REED

THE REED

RELAXED from his tramp in the breathless fir-wood, covered with cobwebs and fir-needles, Meliton Shishkoff, steward at Dementieff's farm, gun on shoulder, walked by the margin of the wood. His Damka, cross between setter and yard-dog, pregnant but unnaturally thin, with wet tail between legs, dragged herself after her master, and did her best to escape being pricked. It was a tedious, cloudy morning. The mist - shrouded trees and bracken scattered big drops, and the damp forest exhaled a smell of decay.

Ahead, where the wood ended, rose birches, and between their trunks and branches gleamed a vision of mist. Some one behind the birches played a home-made shepherd's reed. The musician piped only half a dozen notes, piped them idly, with no attempt at melody, and his music sounded rude and tedious beyond words.

Where the forest thinned and fir-trees mingled with young birches Meliton saw a herd. Hamshackled horses, cows, and sheep wandered between the bushes, and, making the branches crackle, snuffed at the forest grass. Near the edge of the wood, leaning against a wet birch-trunk, stood an old, thin shepherd, capless, in a tattered frieze caftan. Lost in thought, he looked at the ground and piped his reed mechanically.

"Morning, grandfather! God be good!" Meliton greeted him in a thin, hoarse voice, in no way suited to his great height and big, fleshy face. "You play your reed well! Whose are the animals?"

"Artamonoff's," answered the shepherd reluctantly. He thrust his reed into the bosom of his caftan.

"And the wood also is Artamonoff's?" asked Meliton, looking around. "Of course, Artamonoff's . . . I don't know where I am. I scratched my face to pieces in the briers."

He sat down on the wet ground and rolled a cigarette in a piece of newspaper.

Like his liquid voice, everything about Meliton was petty and clashed with his stature, breadth, and fleshy face—his smile, his eyes, his buttons, the cap which barely kept on his solid, close-clipped head. As he spoke and smiled, his clean-shaven, puffy face and his whole figure expressed childishness, timidity, and meekness.

"It's bad weather, God better it!" he said, turning away his head. "The oats are not yet in, and the rain is on us, Lord help us!"

The shepherd looked at the drizzling sky, at the wood, at the steward's soaked clothing, thought, and made no reply.

"The whole summer's been the same . . ." sighed Meliton. "Bad for the muzhiks, and for the quality no consolation. . . ."

Again the shepherd looked at the sky, again he thought, and then began, with pauses, as if chewing each word.

"The whole world goes the same way. . . . You can expect no good."

"But how are things with you?" asked Meliton. He lighted his cigarette. "Have you seen any woodcock broods in Artamonoff's clearing?"

The shepherd was silent. Again he looked at the sky and about him, thought, and blinked his eyes. . . . It was plain that he ascribed no small weight to his own words, and to increase their value delayed them with a certain solemnity. His glance was keen, with the keenness of the old and grave; and the upturned nostrils and saddle-shaped depression in his nose expressed cunning and contempt.

"No, it seems, I saw none," he answered. "Our gamekeeper, Artemka, says that he saw one brood near Pustoshka on Elijah's Day. I expect he lied. Birds are scarce."

"Yes, brother, scarce! . . . Everywhere scarce. Shooting's hardly worth while. . . . There's no game at all, and what there is isn't worth shooting. Little bits of things; it's painful to see them."

Meliton laughed and waved his hand.

"What's happening all over this world makes me laugh. The birds have gone off the rails; they sit so late that some haven't hatched out by Peter's Day."

"All things go the same way," said the shepherd, lifting his face. "Last year game birds were scarce, this year they're scarcer still, and in five years to come—mark my words—there won't be one left! Not only no game, but no birds of any kind."

"That's true," said Meliton thoughtfully. "That's true!"

The shepherd laughed bitterly and shook his head.

"It's a miracle!" he said. "What has become of them all? Twenty years gone by, I remember, there were geese and cranes, ducks and grouse— flocks upon flocks of them! I remember; the squire and his friends would come down and shoot, and all you could hear all day was pu, pu, pu, pu, pu! Plover and snipe without end to them, and little teals and woodcock as common as starlings—or spar- rows, if you will. No end to them! Where are they gone? Even the birds of prey are gone! Gone are the eagles and the hawks and the owls. . . . Beasts of all sorts are few. The wolf and the fox are rare sights to-day, not to mention bears and otters. And in those days there were elks. Forty years I watch the works of God from day to day, and all, I can see it plainly, is going in one way!"

"What way?"

"To the worse, lad. To ruin's the only conclusion. . . . The time is nigh for God's world to perish."

The old man put on his cap and looked up.

"It's a pity!" he sighed after a short silence. "Lord, what a pity! It's God's will, of course—not we made the world, but it's a pity, brother! When a tree is withered, or a cow dies, we're sorry to see it. But what do you say, good man, to the whole world perishing? What good, Lord Jesus? And the sun . . . and the sky, and the woods . . . and the rivers . . . and the beasts—surely all these were made, adapted, fitted to one another. Each for its own work, each in its own place. . . . And all this will perish!"

A mournful smile passed over the shepherd's face, and he blinked his eyes.

"You think the whole world perishes?" said Meliton thoughtfully. "It may be; perhaps we are really near the end. But I don't believe that birds alone prove anything."

"Not birds only," replied the shepherd. "But beasts also . . . and cattle and bees and fish. . . . If you don't believe what I say, ask the old men. They'll tell you that fish are not what they used to be. In the sea, in the lakes, in the rivers, the fish grow less and less. In our Pestchanka, I remember, we caught pike a full yard long. Burbot were every-where, and roach and bream—every fish on earth showed himself sometimes; but now if you catch a nine-inch pike or perch you may thank the Lord. There isn't even a carp left. Every year things get worse and worse, and soon you'll see there'll be no fish at all. . . . And take the rivers of the present day! The rivers are drying up."

"That's true."

"It is. They're shallower and shallower every year; and already, brother, there are no deep pools as there used to be. Do you see those bushes?". The old man pointed aside. "Behind them there's an old channel; in my father's time, the Pestchanka flowed there; but look now, and see where the devil has taken it! It changes its course and will change it till it dries up altogether. And what's become of the smaller streams? In this very wood there was a brook so big that the muzhiks laid nets in it and caught pike; wild ducks wintered there; and now even in flood-time you can't float a boat in it. Yes, brother. Look where you will, everything is bad. Everything!"

The pair were silent. Meliton, lost in thought, stared at one point. He sought but one place in Nature untouched by the all-embracing ruin. On the mist and oblique rain-belts, as on muffed glass, slipped bright spots and at once vanished—the rising sun strove to pierce the clouds and look upon the earth.

"And the forests?" stammered Meliton.

"And the forests," repeated the shepherd. "The forests are cut down, burnt, and dried up, and no new trees grow. What does grow is soon cut down; to-day it is up—to-morrow—look over your shoulder!—and down it's cut. . . . And so on without end until none remain! I, good man, have been watching the village flock ever since the Emancipation, and before that I was shepherd to the squire, shepherd in this very place; and I can't recall a summer day in all my life when I wasn't here. And all those years I observe the world of God. I have seen with my own eyes, brother; and I can tell you that all things that grow are on the way to ruin. Take rye, or oats, or even any flower; they're all on their way to the same end."

"The people, perhaps, are better?" said the steward.

"How better?"

"Cleverer."

"Cleverer maybe. Yes, that's true, but what good is cleverness? What use are brains to people on the brink of ruin? You don't want your brains to die. What good are brains to the sportsman if there is no game? That's just how I reason it: God's given us men brains, and taken away our strength. The people have grown weak, too weak to talk about. Look at me! I have not a kopeck of money;

in all the village, I am the last muzhik.   But all
the same, lad, I have strength.   I am a strong man.
Look at me!   Seventy years I've lived; and I
watch these flocks day after day, yes, and by night
—I watch them for twenty kopecks and never sleep
and never catch cold!   My son is a cleverer man; but
put him in my place, and next day he'll come and
ask for higher wages, or go into hospital.   So it is!
Beyond bread I ask for nothing; it's written, give us
this day our daily bread; but your muzhik nowadays
must have tea and vodka, and white bread, and he
sleeps from sundown to dawn, and drinks medicines,
and is spoilt all round.   And why?   Because he's
weak, he has no strength to endure.   He would like
to do without sleep, but his eyes shut—he's no good
for anything!"

"That's true," said Meliton.   "The muzhik nowadays is good for nothing."

"There's no use hiding it; we get worse every year.
And as for the gentry, they're weaker still than the
muzhiks.   Your gentleman of to-day learns everything
that's no good for him to know.   And what use is
it? . . . Skinny, weak, like some Hungarian or
Frenchman; no dignity, nothing to look at; only
one thing to boast of—he knows he's a gentleman.
He sits with a rod and catches fish, or lies on his back
reading books, or goes among the muzhiks and talks
to them, and when he sees some one hungry hires him

as a clerk. He lives among trifles, and has no real business in him. The old gentry were generals—the new ones are trash!"

"They're impoverished—badly," said Meliton.

"Because God's taken their strength, that's why. You've no chance against God."

Again Meliton stared fixedly at one point. After thinking a moment, he sighed, as sigh grave, sagacious men, shook his head, and said—

"What is the cause? We sin much. . . . We have forgotten God. . . . And now we see the result. The time draws nigh for the end of everything. The world can't last for ever . . . it, too, must have a rest."

The shepherd sighed. He wished, it seemed, to drop a painful subject. He returned to the birches, and began to count the cattle.

"Gei, gei, gei!" he cried. "Gei, gei, gei! I can't abide you. The devil seems to drive you the wrong way."

He glared angrily and went among the bushes to collect his herd. Meliton rose, and walked slowly by the edge of the wood. He looked at the ground, and thought and tried to remember a single thing that was not yet tainted by death. Again on the slant rain-belts slipped bright spots; they quivered in the tree-tops, and were extinguished in the wet leaves. Damka found a hedgehog under a bush, and to call her master's attention, whined.

K

"You had an eclipse, or not?" cried the shepherd from behind the bushes.

"Yes," cried Meliton.

"You had? . . . Everywhere the people complain of it. That means, brother, there's disorder in heaven too. An eclipse isn't sent for nothing. Gei, gei, gei!"

Having got his flock together, the shepherd leaned against a birch-tree, and, looking at the sky, drew the reed idly from his bosom and began to play. He played mechanically as before, keeping to half a dozen notes, as if he handled the reed for the first time; and the notes came forth irresolutely, without order, with no melody imaginable; so that Meliton, deep in thought on the world's coming destruction, found the music painful and unpleasant and wished it would cease. The high, piping notes, which trembled and died away, seemed to weep disconsolately, as if the reed itself were pained and frightened; and the lower notes seemed to speak of the mist, the grey heavens, the melancholy trees. The music, in truth, seemed made for the weather, the old man, and his words.

Meliton felt impelled to complain. He went up to the shepherd, looked at his sad, ironical face and at the reed, and muttered—

"And life has grown worse, grandfather! There's no living nowadays. Famines . . . and poverty . . . murrain, sickness! We are crushed by need."

The steward's puffy face turned purple, and his

expression was feminine and plaintive. He twitched
his fingers, as if seeking words to clothe inexpressible
affliction, and continued—

"Eight children, a wife . . . a mother still alive,
and ten roubles a month for wages, to board myself!
My wife a devil from poverty . . . and I a drunkard!
I am a deliberate, grave man. I want to sit at home
in peace; but all day long, like a dog, I wander about
with my gun . . . because it is more than I can
bear. I hate my home!"

Afraid that his tongue had carried him away, and
that he had said what should be concealed, the
steward waved his hand, and continued bitterly—

"If the world must perish, then let it—the sooner
the better! There's no use delaying it, no use in
suffering without cause. . . ."

The old man took the reed from his lips, and, closing
one eye, looked along it. His face was sad, and covered
with drops as with tears. He smiled and answered—

"It's a pity, brother! Lord, what a pity! The
earth, the woods, the sky . . . the beasts and birds!
. . . all these were made, adapted to their uses,
each has its mind! And all will perish.   . . But
most luckless of all are we men!"

In the forest rustled heavy rain. Meliton looked
towards the sound, buttoned his coat to the neck, and
said—

"I must go back to the village. Good-bye, grandfather! What is your name?"

"Poor Luka."

"Well, good-bye, Luka. Thanks for your good words. Damka! Come!"

Having taken leave of the shepherd, Meliton walked along the wood, and thence through a meadow that gradually merged in a marsh. The water rose in his foot-prints, and the rusty reed-grass bent, as if afraid of his tread. Beyond the marsh, on the banks of the Pestchanka of which grandfather Luka had spoken, rose willows; and behind the willows, in blue patches, stood the squire's barns. The world around presaged the coming of that sad, inevitable time when fields turn dark, when earth grows muddy and cold, when the weeping willow is sadder and down its trunk creep tears, when the crane alone evades the universal wretchedness; and even he, afraid to anger grieved Nature by boasting his delight, fills the air with a tedious, melancholy song.

Meliton walked to the river, and heard the sounds of the reed fading slowly away. He still wished to complain. He looked about him sadly, filled with intolerable pity for the sky, the earth, the sun, the woods, his Damka; and as a high note from the reed whined and trembled past his ears, he felt intense bitterness and offence at the chaos reigning throughout the world.

The high note quivered, and ceased, and the reed was still.

LA CIGALE

LA CIGALE

I

TO Olga Ivanovna's wedding came all her friends and acquaintances.

"Look at him! Isn't it true there is something in him?" she said to them, nodding towards her husband, as if to justify her marriage to this simple, commonplace, in no way remarkable man.

The bridegroom, Osip Stepanuitch Duimoff, was a doctor, with the rank of Titular Councillor. He worked at two hospitals; in one as supernumerary ordinator; as dissector in the other. At one, from nine in the morning till midday, he received out-patients and worked in the wards; and, finished with this, he took a tram to the second hospital, and dissected bodies. His private practice was small, worth some five hundred roubles a year. That was all. What more could be said of him? On the other hand, Olga Ivanovna, her friends and acquaintances, were by no means ordinary. All were noted for something, and fairly well known; they had names; they were celebrated, or if not celebrated yet, they inspired great hope for the future.   A talented actor, clever, modest, a fine gentleman, a master of declamation, who taught Olga Ivanovna to recite ; a good-humoured opera-singer who told Olga Ivanovna with a sigh that she was throwing herself away—if she gave up idling and took herself in hand, she would make a famous singer ; a few artists, chief of them the genre-ist, animal-, and landscape-painter Riabovsky, handsome, fair-haired, twenty-five, successful at exhibitions, who sold his last picture for five hundred roubles—he touched up Olga Ivanovna's *études*, and predicted a future for her; a violoncellist, whose instrument wept, who frankly said that of all the women he knew Olga Ivanovna alone could accompany ; a man of letters, young, but already known for his short stories, sketches, and plays. Who else? Yes, Vassili Vassiluitch, country gentleman, dilettante illustrator and vignettist, with his love of the national epos and his passion for old Russian art—on paper, china, and smoked plates he turned out veritable masterpieces. In such society— artistic, free, and spoiled by fate ; and (though delicate and modest) oblivious of doctors save when ill; to whom " Duimoff" sounded as impersonal as " Tarasoff" or " Sidoroff"—in such society, the bridegroom seemed out-of-place, needless, and even insignificant, although he was really a very tall and very broad-shouldered man. His evening dress seemed made for some one else. His beard was like a shopman's. Though it is true that had he been a writer or artist, this beard would have reminded them of Zola.

The artist told Olga Ivanovna that with her flaxen hair and wedding dress she was a graceful cherry-tree covered with tender, white blossoms in spring.

"No, but listen!" replied Olga Ivanovna, seizing his hand. "How suddenly all this happened!. Listen, listen! . . . I should tell you that Duimoff and my father were at the same hospital. While my poor father was ill, Duimoff watched day and night at his bedside. Such self-sacrifice! Listen, Riabovsky! . . . And you, writer, listen—this is very interesting! Come nearer! Such sacrifice of self, such sincere concern! I myself could not sleep at night, and sat at my father's bedside, and suddenly! . . . I captivated the poor young man! My Duimoff was up to his neck in love! In truth, things happen strangely. Well, after my father's death we sometimes met in the street; he paid me occasional visits, and one fine evening suddenly— he proposed to me! . . . I cried all night, and myself fell in love with him. And now, you see, I am married. Don't you think there is something in him? Something strong, mighty, leonine! Just now his face is turned three-quarters from us and the light is bad, but when he turns round just look at his fore-head! Riabovsky, what do you think of his forehead? Duimoff, we are speaking of you." She turned to her husband. "Come here! Give your honest hand to Riabovsky. . . . That's right. Be friends!"

With a simple, kindly smile, Duimoff gave his hand to the artist, and said—

"I'm delighted! There was a Riabovsky at college with me. Was he a relation of yours?"

II

Olga Ivanovna was twenty-two years old, Duimoff thirty-one. After the marriage they lived well. Olga Ivanovna hung the drawing-room with drawings, her own and her friends', framed and unframed ; and about the piano and furniture, arranged in pretty confusion Chinese parasols, easels, many-coloured draperies, poniards, busts, photographs. The dining-room she decked with the bright-coloured oleographs beloved by peasants, bast-shoes and sickles, and these, with the scythe and hay-rake in the corner, made a room in national style. To make her bedroom like a cave, she draped the ceiling and walls with dark cloth, hung a Venetian lantern over the bed, and set near the door a figure with a halberd. And every one agreed that the young couple had a charming flat.

Rising every day at eleven, Olga Ivanovna sat at the piano, or, if the sun shone, painted in oils. At one o'clock she drove to her dressmaker's. As neither she nor Duimoff was rich, many ingenious shifts were resorted to to keep her in the new-looking dresses which made such an impression on all. Pieces of old dyed cloth ; worthless patches of tulle, lace, plush, and silk, came back from the dressmaker miracles, not dresses but ravishing dreams. Done with the dressmaker, Olga Ivanovna drove to some actress friend to learn theatrical news and get tickets for first-nights or benefits ; thence to an artist's studio or picture gallery, ending up with some other celebrity whom she invited to visit her, or simply gossiped to. And those whom she counted celebrities and great men received her as an equal, and told her in one voice that if she did not throw away her opportunities, her talents, taste, and intellect would yield something really great. She sang, played, painted, modelled, acted in amateur theatricals; and did everything well : if she merely made lanterns for illuminations, or dressed herself up, or tied some one's necktie, the result was invariably graceful, artistic, charming. But none of her talents outshone her skill in meeting and getting on terms of intimacy with men of note. Let a man get the least reputation, or even be talked about, and in a single day she had met him, established friendly relations, and invited him to her home. And each new acquaintance was a festival in himself. She worshipped the well-known, was proud of them, and dreamed of them all night. Her thirst was insatiable. The old

celebrities departed and were forgotten, and new
celebrities replaced them; and to these last she grew
accustomed in time; they lost their charm, so that
she sought for more.

She dined at home with her husband at five o'clock.
She was in ecstasies over his simplicity, common sense,
and good humour. She jumped up from her chair,
embraced his head, and covered it with kisses.

"You are a clever, a noble man, Duimoff!" she
exclaimed. "You have only one drawback. You take
no interest in art. You deny music and painting."

"I don't understand them," he answered kindly.
"All my life I have studied only science and medicine.
I have no time for art."

"But that is awful, Duimoff!"

"Why awful? Your friends know nothing of science
or medicine, yet you don't blame them for that. To
each man his own! I don't understand landscapes or
operas, but I look at the matter thus: if talented men
devote their lives to such things, and clever men pay
vast sums for them, that means they are useful. I
don't understand them, but not to understand does not
mean to deny."

"Give me your hand! Let me press your honest
hand!"

After dinner Olga Ivanovna drove away to her
friends; after that followed theatres or concerts. She
returned after midnight. And so every day.

On Wednesdays she gave evening parties. There were no cards and no dancing. Hostess and guests devoted themselves to art. The actor recited, the singer sang, artists sketched in Olga Ivanovna's numberless albums; the hostess painted, modelled, accompanied, and sang. In the pauses between these recreations, they talked of books, the theatre, and art. No women were present, because Olga Ivanovna considered all women, except actresses and dressmakers, tiresome and contemptible. When the hall bell rang the hostess started, and exclaimed triumphantly, "It's he!" meaning thereby some newly met celebrity. Duimoff kept out of sight, and few remembered his existence. But at half-past eleven the dining-room door flew open, and Duimoff appeared with a kindly smile, rubbed his hands, and said—

"Come, gentlemen, to supper!"

Whereupon all thronged to the dining-room, and each time found awaiting them the same things: a dish of oysters, a joint of ham or veal, sardines, cheese, caviare, mushrooms, vodka, and two decanters of wine.

"My dear *maître d'hôtel!*" cried Olga Ivanovna, waving her hands ecstatically. "You are simply adorable! Gentlemen, look at his forehead! Duimoff, show us your profile. Look at him, gentlemen: it is the face of a Bengal tiger with an expression as kind and good as a deer's. My sweetheart!"

And the guests ate steadily and looked at Duimoff.

But soon they forgot his presence, and returned to theatre, music, and art.

The young couple were happy. Their life, it seemed, flowed as smoothly as oil. But the third week of the honeymoon was crossed by a cloud. Duimoff got erysipelas at the hospital, and his fine black hair was cut off. Olga Ivanovna sat with him and cried bitterly, but when he got better she bound a white handkerchief around his head and sketched him as a Bedouin. And both were happy. Three days after he had returned to hospital a second misfortune occurred.

"I am in bad luck, mama!" he said at dinner. "To-day I had four dissections, and I cut two fingers. I noticed it only just now."

Olga Ivanovna was frightened. But Duimoff smiled, dismissed the accident as a trifle, and said that he cut himself often.

"I am carried away by my work, mama, and forget what I'm about."

Olga Ivanovna dreaded blood-poisoning, and at night prayed to God. But no consequences followed, and life, serene and happy, flowed without trouble or alarm. The present was all delight, and behind it came spring—spring already near, beaming and beckoning, with a thousand joys. Pleasures it promised without end. In April, May, and June a villa far from town, with walks, fishing, studies, nightingales.

From June till autumn the artists' tour on the Volga,
and in this tour, as member of the Artists' Associa-
tion, Olga Ivanovna would take part. She had
already ordered two expensive dresses of gingham,
and laid in a stock of colours, brushes, canvas, and
a new palette. Almost every day came Riabovsky
to watch her progress in painting. When she showed
him her work he thrust his hands deep in his pockets,
compressed tightly his lips, grunted, and said—

"So! . . . This cloud of yours glares; the light
is not right for evening. The foreground is somehow
chewed up, and there is something, you understand.
. . . And the cabin is somehow crushed . . . you
should make that corner a little darker. But on the
whole it's not bad. . . . I can praise it."

And the less intelligibly he spoke the better Olga
Ivanovna understood.

III

After dinner, on the second day of Trinity week,
Duimoff bought some *hors d'œuvres* and sweets and
took train for his villa in the country. Two whole
weeks he had not seen his wife, and he longed to be
with her again. During the journey and afterwards,
as he searched for the villa in a big wood, he felt
hungry and fatigued, and rejoiced at the thought of

supping in freedom with his wife and having a sound sleep. So, looking at his parcel of caviare, cheese, and white-fish, he felt happy.

Before he found the villa the sun had begun to set. The old servant said that her mistress was not at home, but that she would soon return. The villa, a very ugly villa, with low ceilings, papered with writing-paper, and uneven, chinky floors, contained only three rooms. In one was a bed, in another canvas, brushes, dirty paper, and men's clothes and hats scattered on chairs and window-sills; and in the third Duimoff found three strangers, two dark and bearded, the third—evidently an actor—clean-shaven and stout.

"What do you want?" asked the actor in a bass voice, looking at Duimoff shyly. "You want Olga Ivanovna? Wait; she'll be back shortly."

Duimoff sat down and waited. One of the dark men, looking at him drowsily and lazily, poured tea into his glass and asked—

"Would you like some tea?"

Duimoff wanted both to eat and drink, but, fearing to spoil his appetite, he refused the tea. Soon afterwards came footsteps and a familiar laugh; the door flew open, and in came Olga Ivanovna wearing a big hat. On her arm hung a basket, and behind her, with a big parasol and a deck-chair, came merry, rosy-cheeked Riabovsky.

"Duimoff!" cried Olga Ivanovna, radiant with joy. "Duimoff!" she repeated, laying her head and both hands on his shoulder. "It is you? Why did you not come sooner? Why? Why?"

"I couldn't, mama! I am always busy, and when I end my work there's generally no train."

"How glad I am you've come! I dreamed of you all, all last night. *Akh*, if you knew how I love you —and how opportunely you've come! You are my saviour! To-morrow we have a most original wedding." She laughed and re-tied her husband's tie. "A young telegraphist at the station, a certain Tchik-eldeyeff, is going to be married. A handsome boy, not at all stupid; in his face, you know, there's something strong, bearish. . . . He'd sit admirably as model for a Varangian. We are all interested in him, and promised to come to the wedding. . . . He is a poor man, solitary and shy, and it would be a sin to refuse. Imagine! . . . after church there'll be the wedding, then all go to the bride's house . . . you understand . . . the woods, the birds' songs, sun-spots on the grass, and we ourselves—variegated spots on a bright green background. . . . Most original, quite in the style of the French impressionists! But what am I to wear, Duimoff? I have nothing here, literally nothing. . . . No dress, no flowers, no gloves! . . . You must save me. Your arrival means that fate is on my side. Here are the keys, sweet-

L

heart! take the train home and bring my rose-coloured dress from the wardrobe. You know it; it's the first you'll see. Then in the chest of drawers—the bottom right-hand drawer—you'll find two boxes. At the top there's only tulle and other rags, but underneath you'll find flowers. Bring all the flowers— carefully! I don't know . . . then I'll choose. . . . And buy me some gloves."

"All right," said Duimoff. "I'll get them to-morrow!"

"How to-morrow?" asked Olga Ivanovna, looking at him with surprise. "You can't do it to-morrow. The first train leaves at nine, and the wedding is at eleven. No, dear; go to-night! If you can't get back yourself to-morrow send a messenger. The train is nearly due. Don't miss it, my soul!"

"All right!"

"*Akh*, how sorry I am to have to send you!" she said, and tears came into her eyes. "Why did I promise the telegraph clerk, like a fool!"

Duimoff hastily gulped down a glass of tea, and, still smiling kindly, returned to the station. And the caviare, the cheese, and the white-fish were eaten by the actor and the two dark men.

IV

It was a still moonlight night of July. Olga Ivanovna stood on the deck of a Volga steamer and looked now at the river, now at its beautiful banks. Beside her stood Riabovsky, and affirmed that the black shadows on the water were not shadows but a dream; that this magic stream with its fantastic shimmer, this unfathomable sky, these mournful banks—which expressed but the vanity of life, and the existence of something higher, something eternal, something blessed —called to us to forget ourselves, to die, to fade into memories. The past was trivial and tedious, the future insignificant; and this magic night, this one night of life, would soon be past, would have hurried into eternity. Why, then, live?

And Olga Ivanovna listened, first to Riabovsky's voice, then to the midnight silence, and thought that she was immortal, and would never die. The river's turquoise hue, a hue she had never seen before, the sky, the banks, the black shadows, and the irresponsible joy which filled her heart, all whispered to her that she would become a great artist, that somewhere far away, beyond these distances, beyond the moonlight night, somewhere in infinite space there awaited success and glory, and the love of the world. When she looked earnestly into the distance, she saw crowds, lights; she heard solemn music and cries of rapture; she saw herself in a white dress surrounded by flowers cast at her from all sides. And she believed that here beside her, leaning on the bulwark, stood a really great man, a genius, the elected of God. He had already accomplished things beautiful, new, uncommon; what he would do when time had ripened his great talents would be greater immeasurably—that was written legibly in his face, his expressions, his relations to the world around. Of the shadows, the hues of nights, the moonlight, he spoke in language all his own, and unconsciously betrayed the power of his magic mastery over Nature. He was handsome and original; and his life, unhampered, free, alien to the trifles of the world, seemed the life of a bird.

"It is getting cold!" said Olga Ivanovna, shuddering.

Riabovsky wrapped her in his cloak and said mournfully—

"I feel myself in your power. I am a slave. Why are you so ravishing to-night?"

He looked at her steadily, and his eyes were so terrible that she feared to look at him.

"I love you madly . . ." he whispered, breathing against her cheek. "Say to me but one word, and I will not live . . . I will abandon my art. . . ." He stammered in his extreme agitation. "Love me, love. . . ."

"Don't speak in that way!" said Olga Ivanovna, closing her eyes. "It is terrible. And Duimoff?"

"What is Duimoff? Why Duimoff? What have I to do with Duimoff? The Volga, the moon, beauty, my love, my raptures . . . and no Duimoff at all! . . . *Akh*, I know nothing. . . . I do not want the past; give me but one moment . . . one second!"

Olga Ivanovna's heart beat quickly. She tried to think of her husband; but her whole past, her marriage, Duimoff, even the evening parties seemed to her trivial, contemptible, dull, needless, and remote. . . . And, indeed, who was Duimoff? Why Duimoff? What had she to do with Duimoff? Did he exist really in Nature; was he only a dream?

"He has had more happiness than he could expect, a simple and ordinary man," she thought, closing her eyes. "Let them condemn me, let them curse me; but I will take all and perish, take all and perish. . . . We must experience everything in life. . . . Lord, how painful and how good!"

"Well, what? What?" stammered the artist, embracing her. He kissed her hands greedily, while she strove to withdraw them. "You love me? Yes? Yes? O, what a night! O night divine!"

"Yes, what a night!" she whispered, looking into his eyes which glittered with tears. Then she looked around her, clasped her arms about him, and kissed him firmly on the lips.

"We are near Kineshma," said a voice somewhere across the deck.

Heavy footfalls echoed behind them. A waiter passed from the buffet.

"Waiter!" cried Olga Ivanovna, laughing and crying in her joy. "Bring us some wine."

Pale with excitement, the artist sat on a bench, and stared at Olga Ivanovna with grateful, adoring eyes. But in a moment he shut these eyes, and said with a weary smile—

"I am tired."

And he leaned his head against the bulwark.

V

The second of September was warm and windless but dull. Since early morning a light mist had wandered across the Volga, and at nine o'clock it began to rain. There was no hope of a clear sky. At breakfast Riabovsky told Olga Ivanovna that painting was the most thankless and tedious of arts, that he was no artist, and that only fools thought him talented. Then, for no cause whatever, he seized a knife and cut to pieces his best study. After breakfast, in bad humour, he sat at a window and looked at the river, and found it without life—dull, dead, and cold. All around spoke of frowning autumn's approach. It seemed already that the green carpet on the banks, the diamond flashes from the water, the clear

blue distances—all the vanity and parade of Nature had
been taken from the Volga and packed in a box
until the coming spring; and that the ravens flying
over the river mocked it and cried, "Naked! Naked!"
Riabovsky listened to their cry, and brooded on the
exhaustion and loss of his talent: and he thought
that all the world was conditional, relative, and
stupid, and that he should not have tied himself up
with this woman. In one word he was out of spirits,
and sulked.

On her bed behind the partition, pulling at her
pretty hair, sat Olga Ivanovna; and pictured herself
at home, first in the drawing-room, then in her bedroom, then in her husband's study; imagination bore
her to theatres, to her dressmaker, to her friends.
What was Duimoff doing now? Did he think of her?
The season had already begun; it was time to think
of the evening parties. And Duimoff? Dear Duimoff!
How kindly, with what infantile complaints, he
begged her in his letters to come home! Every
month he sent her seventy-five roubles, and when she
wrote that she had borrowed a hundred from the
artists he sent her also that hundred. The good, the
generous man! Olga Ivanovna was tired of the tour;
she suffered from tedium, and wished to escape as soon
as possible from the muzhiks, from the river damp,
from the feeling of physical uncleanliness caused by
living in huts and wandering from village to village.

Had Riabovsky not promised his brother artists to stay till the twentieth of September, they might have left at once.   And how good it would be to leave!

" My God ! " groaned Riabovsky. " Will the sun ever come out ? I cannot paint a landscape without the sun ! "

" But your study of a cloudy sky ? " said Olga Ivanovna, coming from behind the partition. " You remember, the one with the trees in the foreground to the right, and the cows and geese at the left.   You could finish that."

" What ? " The artist frowned. " Finish it ? Do you really think I'm so stupid that I don't know what to do ? "

" What I do think is that you've changed to me ! " sighed Olga Ivanovna.

" Yes ; and that's all right."

Olga Ivanovna's face quivered ; she went to the stove and began to cry.

" We only wanted tears to complete the picture! Do stop ! I have a thousand reasons for crying, but I don't cry."

" A thousand reasons ! " burst out Olga Ivanovna. " The chief reason is that you are tired of me.   Yes ! " She began to sob. " I will tell you the truth : you are ashamed of your love. You try to hide it, to prevent the others noticing, but that is useless, because they knew about it long ago."

"Olga, I ask only one thing," said the artist
imploringly. He put his hand to his ear. "One
thing only; do not torture me! I want nothing more
from you!"

"Then swear to me that you love me still!"

"This is torture!" hissed Riabovsky through his
teeth. He jumped up. "It will end in my throwing
myself into the Volga, or going out of my mind.
Leave me alone!"

"Then kill me! Kill me!" cried Olga Ivanovna.
"Kill me!"

She again sobbed, and retired behind the partition.
Raindrops pattered on the cabin roof. Riabovsky
with his hands to his head walked from corner to
corner; then with a determined face, as if he wanted
to prove something, put on his cap, took his gun, and
went out of the hut.

When he left, Olga Ivanovna lay on her bed and
cried. At first she thought that it would be good to
take poison, so that Riabovsky on his return would
find her dead. But soon her thoughts bore her back
to the drawing-room and to her husband's study; and
she fancied herself sitting quietly beside Duimoff,
enjoying physical rest and cleanliness; and spending
the evening listening to *Cavalleria Rusticana*. And
a yearning for civilisation, for the sound of cities, for
celebrities filled her heart. A peasant woman entered
the hut, and lazily prepared the stove for dinner.

There was a smell of soot, and the air turned blue from smoke. Then in came several artists in muddy top boots, their faces wet with rain; and they looked at the drawings, and consoled themselves by saying that even in bad weather the Volga had its especial charm. The cheap clock on the wall ticked away; half-frozen flies swarmed in the ikon-corner and buzzed; and cockroaches could be heard under the benches.

Riabovsky returned at sunset. He flung his cap on the table, and, pale, tired, and muddy, dropped on a bench and shut his eyes.

"I am tired," he said, and wrinkled his brows, trying to open his eyes.

To show him kindness, and prove that her anger had passed, Olga Ivanovna came up to him, kissed him silently, and drew a comb through his long, fair hair.

"What are you doing?" he asked, starting as if something cold had touched him. He opened his eyes. "What are you doing? Leave me alone, I beg of you!"

He repulsed her with both hands; and his face seemed to express repugnance and vexation. The peasant woman cautiously brought him a plate, and Olga Ivanovna noticed how she stuck her big fingers in the soup. And the dirty peasant woman with her pendent stomach, the soup which Riabovsky ate greedily, the hut, which she had loved at first for its plainness and artistic disorder, seemed to her unbearable. She felt a deep sense of offence, and said coldly—

"We must part for a time, otherwise we'll only quarrel seriously out of sheer tedium. I am tired of this. I am going to-day."

"Going, how? On the steamer?"

"To-day is Thursday—there is a steamer at half-past nine."

"Eh? Yes! . . . All right, go," said Riabovsky softly, using a towel for a table-napkin. "It's tiresome here for you, and there's nothing to do. Only a great egoist would try to keep you. Go . . . we will meet after the twentieth."

Olga Ivanovna, in good spirits, packed her clothes. Her cheeks burnt with pleasure. "Is it possible?" she asked herself. "Is it possible I shall soon paint in the drawing-room and sleep in a bedroom and dine off a tablecloth?" Her heart grew lighter, and her anger with the artist disappeared.

"I'll leave you the colours and brushes, Riabusha," she said. "You'll bring everything. . . . And, mind, don't idle when I am gone; don't sulk, but work. You are my boy, Riabusha!"

At ten o'clock Riabovsky kissed her good-bye in the hut, to avoid—as she saw—kissing her on the landing-stage in the presence of others. Soon afterwards the steamer arrived and took her away.

Two and a half days later she reached home. Still in her hat and waterproof cloak, panting with excitement, she went through the drawing-room into the dining-room. In his shirt-sleeves, with unbuttoned waistcoat, Duimoff sat at the table and sharpened a knife; on a plate before him was a grouse. As Olga Ivanovna entered the house she resolved to hide the truth from her husband, and felt that she was clever and strong enough to succeed. But when she saw his broad, kindly, happy smile and his bright, joyful eyes, she felt that to deceive such a man would be base and impossible, as impossible as to slander, steal, or kill; and she made up her mind in a second to tell him the whole story. When he had kissed and embraced her she fell upon her knees and hid her face.

"What? What is it, mama?" he asked tenderly. "You got tired of it?"

She raised her face, red with shame, and looked at him guiltily and imploringly. But fear and shame forbade her to tell the truth.

"It is nothing," she said. "I only . . ."

"Sit down here!" he said, lifting her and seating her at the table. "There we are! Eat the grouse! You are starving, of course, poor child!"

She breathed in greedily her native air and ate the grouse. And Duimoff looked at her with rapture and smiled merrily.

VI

Apparently about the middle of winter Duimoff first suspected his wife's unfaithfulness. He behaved as if his own conscience reproached him. He no longer looked her straight in the face; no longer smiled radiantly when she came in sight; and, to avoid being alone with her, often brought home to dinner his colleague, Korosteleff, a little short-haired man, with a crushed face, who showed his confusion in Olga Ivanovna's society by buttoning and un-buttoning his coat and pinching his right moustache. During dinner the doctors said that when the diaphragm rises abnormally high the heart sometimes beats irregularly, that neuritis had greatly increased, and they discussed Duimoff's discovery made during dis-section that a case of cancer of the pancreas had been wrongly diagnosed as "malignant anæmia." And it was plain that both men spoke only of medicine in order that Olga Ivanovna might be silent and tell no lies. After dinner, Korosteleff sat at the piano, and Duimoff sighed and said to him—

"*Akh*, brother! Well! Play me something mournful."

Whereupon, raising his shoulders and spreading his hands, Korosteleff strummed a few chords and sang in tenor, "Show me but one spot where Russia's peasants do not groan!" and Duimoff sighed again, rested his head on his hands, and seemed lost in thought.

Of late Olga Ivanovna had behaved recklessly. She awoke each morning in bad spirits, tortured by the thought that Riabovsky no longer loved her, that—thanks to the Lord, all the same!—all was over. But as she drank her coffee she reasoned that Riabovsky had stolen her from her husband, and that now she belonged to neither. Then she remembered a friend's remark that Riabovsky was getting ready for the exhibition a striking picture, a mixture of landscape and *genre*, in the style of Polienoff, and that this picture sent every one into raptures; this, she consoled herself, he had done under her influence. Thanks to her influence, indeed, he had on the whole changed for the better, and deprived of it, he would probably perish. She remembered that when last he visited her he came in a splashed cloth coat and a new tie and asked her languidly, "Am I good-looking?" And, in truth, elegant Riabovsky with his blue eyes and long curls was very good-looking—or, it may be, he merely seemed so—and he had treated her with affection.

Having remembered and reasoned much, Olga Ivanovna dressed, and in deep agitation drove to Riabovsky's studio. He was in good humour, delighted with what was indeed a fine picture ; he hopped, played

the fool, and answered every serious question with a
joke. Olga Ivanovna was jealous of the picture, and
hated it, but for the sake of good manners, she stood
before it five minutes, and, sighing as people sigh
before holy things, said softly—

" Yes, you never painted like that before. Do you
know, it almost frightens me."

And she began to implore him to love her, not to
forsake her, to pity her—poor and unfortunate! She
kissed his hand, cried, made him swear his love, and
boasted that without her influence he would go off the
track and perish utterly. Thus having spoilt his good
humour, and humiliated herself, she would drive away
to a dressmaker, or to some actress friend to ask for free
tickets.

Once when she found Riabovsky out she left a note
swearing that if he did not visit her at once she would
take poison. And he, frightened, came and stayed to
dinner. Ignoring her husband's presence, he spoke to
her impudently; and she answered in the same tone.
They felt chained to one another; they were despots
and foes; and their anger hid from them their own
rudeness, which even close-clipped Korosteleff remarked.
After dinner Riabovsky said good-bye hastily and
went.

" Where are you going?" asked Olga Ivanovna.
She stood in the hall, and looked at him with hatred.

Riabovsky frowned and blinked, and named a woman

she knew, and it was plain that he enjoyed her jealousy, and wished to annoy her. Olga Ivanovna went to her bedroom and lay on her bed; from jealousy, anger, and a sense of humiliation and shame, she bit her pillow, and sobbed aloud. Duimoff left Korosteleff alone, came into the bedroom, and, confused and abstracted, said softly—

"Don't cry so loudly, mama! . . . What good is it? We must keep silence about this. . . . People mustn't see. . . . You know yourself that what has happened is beyond recall."

Unable to appease the painful jealousy which made her temples throb, thinking, nevertheless, that what had happened was not beyond recall, she washed and powdered her face, and flew off to the woman friend. Finding no Riabovsky there she drove to another, then to a third. . . . At first she felt ashamed of these visits, but she soon reconciled herself; and one evening even called on every woman she knew and sought Riabovsky; and all of them understood her.

Of her husband she said to Riabovsky—

"This man tortures me with his magnanimity."

And this sentence so pleased her that, meeting artists who knew of her affair with Riabovsky, she repeated with an emphatic gesture—

"This man tortures me with his magnanimity."

In general, her life remained unchanged. She resumed her Wednesday-evening parties. The actor declaimed, the painters sketched, the violoncellist played, the singers sang; and invariably half an hour before midnight the dining-room door opened, and Duimoff said with a smile—

"Come, gentlemen, supper is ready."

As before, Olga Ivanovna sought celebrities, found them, and, insatiable, sought for more. As before, she returned home late. But Duimoff, no longer sleeping as of old, sat in his study and worked. He went to bed at three, and rose at eight.

Once as she stood before the pier-glass dressing for the theatre, Duimoff, in evening dress and a white tie, came into the room. He smiled kindly, with his old smile, and looked his wife joyfully in the face. His face shone.

"I have just defended my dissertation," he said. He sat down and stroked his leg.

"Your dissertation?" said Olga Ivanovna.

"Yes," he laughed. He stretched forward so as to see in the mirror the face of his wife, who continued to stand with her back to him and dress her hair. "Yes," he repeated. "Do you know what? I expect to be offered a privat-docentship in general pathology. That is something."

It was plain from his radiant face that had Olga Ivanovna shared his joy and triumph he would have forgiven and forgotten everything. But "privat-docentship" and "general pathology" had no meaning

M

for her, and, what's more, she feared to be late for the theatre. She said nothing.

Duimoff sat still for a few minutes, smiled guiltily, and left the room.

VII

This was an evil day.

Duimoff's head ached badly; he ate no breakfast, and did not go to the hospital, but lay on the sofa in his study. At one o'clock Olga Ivanovna went to Riabovsky's, to show him her *Nature morte*, and ask why he had not come the day before. The *Nature morte* she herself did not take seriously; she had painted it only as an excuse to visit the artist.

She went to his apartment unannounced. As she took off her goloshes in the hall she heard hasty footsteps, and the rustle of a woman's dress; and as she hurried into the studio a brown skirt flashed for a moment before her and vanished behind a big picture, which together with its easel was hung with black calico. There was no doubt that a woman hid there. How often had Olga Ivanovna herself hidden behind that picture! Riabovsky, in confusion, stretched out both hands as if surprised at her visit, and said with a constrained smile—

"Ah, I am glad to see you. What is the news?"

Olga Ivanovna's eyes filled with tears. She was

ashamed and angered, and would have given millions
to be spared speaking before the strange woman, the
rival, the liar, who hid behind the picture and
tittered, no doubt, maliciously.

"I have brought a study . . ." she said in a thin,
frightened voice. Her lips trembled. "*Nature morte.*"

"What? What? A study?"

The artist took the sketch, looked at it, and walked
mechanically into another room. Olga Ivanovna
followed submissively.

"*Nature morte* . . ." he stammered, seeking rhymes.
"*Kurort . . . sort . . . porte . . .*"

From the studio came hasty footfalls and the rustle
of a skirt. She had gone. Olga Ivanovna felt impelled to scream and strike the artist on the head; but
tears blinded her, she was crushed by her shame, and
felt as if she were not Olga Ivanovna the artist, but
a little beetle.

"I am tired . . ." said Riabovsky languidly. He
looked at the study, and shook his head as if to drive
away sleep. "This is charming, of course, but . . .
it is study to-day, and study to-morrow, and study
last year, and study it will be again in a month. . . .
How is it you don't get tired? If I were you, I
should give up painting, and take up seriously music,
or something else. . . . You are not an artist but a
musician. You cannot imagine how tired I am.
Let me order some tea. Eh?"

He left the room, and Olga Ivanovna heard him giving an order. To avoid good-byes and explanations, still more to prevent herself sobbing, she went quickly into the hall, put on her goloshes, and went out. Once in the street she sighed faintly. She felt that she was for ever rid of Riabovsky and painting, and the heavy shame which had crushed her in the studio. All was over! She drove to her dressmaker, then to Barnay, who had arrived the day before, and from Barnay to a music shop, thinking all the time how she would write Riabovsky a cold, hard letter, full of her own worth; and that the spring and summer she would spend with Duimoff in the Crimea, free herself for ever from the past, and begin life anew.

On her return, late as usual, she sat in her street clothes in the drawing-room, and prepared to write. Riabovsky had told her she was no artist; in revenge she would write that he painted every year one and the same tiresome thing, that he had exhausted himself, and would never again produce original work. She would write also that he owed much to her beneficent influence; and that if he made mistakes it was only because her influence was paralysed by various ambiguous personages who hid behind his pictures.

"Mama!" cried Duimoff from his study, without opening the door.

"What is it?"

"Mama, don't come in, but just come to the door.

It is this. The day before yesterday I took diphtheria at the hospital, and now . . . I feel bad. Send at once for Korosteleff."

Olga Ivanovna called her husband and men-friends by their surnames; she disliked his name Osip, which reminded her of Gogol's Osip, and the pun " *Osip okrip, a Arkhip osip.*" But this time she cried—

" Osip, that is impossible ! "

" Send! I am ill," said Duimoff from behind the door; and she heard him walking to the sofa and lying down. " Send ! " came his hoarse voice.

" What can it be," thought Olga Ivanovna, chilled with fear. " Why this is dangerous ! "

Without any aim she took a candle, and went into her room, and there, wondering what she should do, she saw herself unexpectedly in the glass. With her pale, terrified face, her high-sleeved jacket with the yellow gathers on the breast, her skirt with its strange stripes, she seemed to herself frightful and repulsive. And suddenly she felt sorry for Duimoff, sorry for his infinite love, his young life, the forsaken bed on which he had not slept so long. And remembering his kindly, suppliant smile, she cried bitterly, and wrote Korosteleff an imploring letter. It was two o'clock in the morning.

VIII

When at eight next morning Olga Ivanovna, heavy from sleeplessness, untidy, unattractive, and guilty-faced, came out of her bedroom, an unknown, black-bearded man, obviously a doctor, passed her in the hall. There was a smell of drugs. Outside Duimoff's study stood Korosteleff, twisting his left moustache with his right hand.

"Excuse me, I cannot let you in," he said, looking at her savagely. "You might catch the disease. And in any case, what's the use? He's raving."

"Is it really diphtheria?" whispered Olga Ivanovna.

"People who do foolish things ought to pay for them," muttered Korosteleff, ignoring Olga Ivanovna's question. "Do you know how he got this diphtheria? On Tuesday he sucked through a tube the diphtheria laminæ from a boy's throat. And why? Stupid. . . . Like a fool!"

"Is it dangerous? Very?" asked she.

"Yes, it's a very bad form, they say. We must send for Schreck, we must. . . ."

First came a little, red-haired, long-nosed man with a Jewish accent; then a tall, stooping, untidy man like a proto-deacon; lastly a young, very stout, red-faced man with spectacles. All these doctors came to attend their sick colleague. Korosteleff, having

served his turn, remained in the house, wandering
about like a shadow. The maid-servant was kept
busy serving the doctors with tea, and running to
the apothecary's, and no one tidied the rooms. All
was still and sad.

. Olga Ivanovna sat in her room, and reflected that
God was punishing her for deceiving her husband.
That silent, uncomplaining, inexplicable man—imper-
sonified, it seemed, by kindness and mildness, weak
from excessive goodness—lay on his sofa and suffered
alone, uttering no groan. And if he did complain
in his delirium, the doctors would guess that the
diphtheria was not the only culprit. They would
question Korostcleff, who knew all, and not without
cause looked viciously at his friend's wife as if she
were chief and real offender, and disease only her
accomplice. She no longer thought of the moonlight Volga night, the love avowal, the romance of
life in the peasant's hut; she remembered only that
from caprice and selfishness she had smeared herself
from head to feet with something vile and sticky
which no washing would wash away.

"*Akh*, how I lied to him!" she said, remembering her restless love of Riabovsky. "May it be
accursed!"

At four o'clock she dined with Korosteleff, who
ate nothing, but drank red wine, and frowned. She
too ate nothing. But she prayed silently, and vowed

to God that if Duimoff only recovered, she would love him again and be his faithful wife. Then, forgetting herself for a moment, she looked at Korosteleff and thought: "How tiresome it is to be such a simple, undistinguished, obscure man, and to have such bad manners." It seemed to her that God would strike her dead for her cowardice in keeping away from her husband. And altogether she was oppressed by a dead melancholy, and a feeling that her life was ruined, and that nothing now would mend it.

After dinner, darkness. Olga Ivanovna went into the drawing-room, and found Korosteleff asleep on a couch, his head resting on a silk cushion embroidered with gold. He snored loudly.

Alone the doctors, coming on and off duty, ignored the disorder. The strange man sleeping and snoring in the drawing-room, the studies on the walls, the wonderful decorations, the mistress's dishevelled hair and untidy dress—none of these awakened the least interest. One of the doctors laughed; and this laugh had such a timid sound that it was painful to hear.

When next Olga Ivanovna entered the drawing-room Korosteleff was awake. He sat up and smoked.

"He has got diphtheria . . . in the nasal cavity," he said quietly. "Yes . . . and his heart is weak. . . . It is a bad business."

"Better send for Schreck," said Olga Ivanovna,

"He's been. It was he noticed that the diphtheria had got into the nose. Yes . . . but what is Schreck? In reality, Schreck is nothing. He is Schreck, I am Korosteleff, and nothing more!"

Time stretched into eternity. Olga Ivanovna lay dressed on her unmade bed, and slumbered. She felt that the whole flat from floor to ceiling was filled with a giant block of iron, and that if the iron were only removed, all would be well again. But then she remembered that there was no iron, but only Duimoff's illness.

"*Nature morte* . . ." she thought, again losing consciousness. "Sport, *kurort*. . . . And what about Schreck? Schreck, greck, vreck, kreck. Where are my friends now? Do they know of the sorrow that has overtaken us? O Lord, save . . . deliver us! Schreck, greck. . . ."

And again the iron. Time stretched into eternity, and the clock downstairs struck innumerable times. Now and then the bell was rung. Doctors came. . . . In came the servant with an empty glass on a salver, and said—

"Shall I make the bed, ma'am?"

And, receiving no answer, she went out. Again the clock struck—dreams of rain on the Volga—and again some one arrived, this time, it seemed, a stranger. Olga Ivanovna started, and saw Korosteleff.

"What time is it?" she asked.

"About three."

"Well, what?"

"Just that. I came to say that he's dying."

He sobbed, sat down on her bed, and wiped away his tears with his sleeve. At first Òlga Ivanovna understood nothing; than she turned cold, and began to cross herself.

"He is dying," he repeated in a thin voice; and again he sobbed. "He is dying—because he sacrificed himself. What a loss to science!" He spoke bitterly. "This man, compared with the best of us, was a great man, an exceptional man! What gifts! What hopes he awakened in us all!" Korosteleff wrung his hands. "Lord, my God, you will not find such a scholar if you search till judgment day! Oska Duimoff, Oska Duimoff, what have you done? My God!"

In despair he covered his face with his hands and shook his head.

"And what moral fortitude!" he continued, each second increasing in anger. "Good, pure, loving soul— not a man, but a crystal! How he served his science, how he's died for it. Worked—day and night—like an ox, sparing himself never; and he, the young scholar, the coming professor, was forced to seek a practice and spend his nights translating to pay for these . . . these dirty rags!"

Korosteleff looked fiendishly at Olga Ivanovna, seized the sheet with both hands, and tore it as angrily as if it, and not she, were guilty.

"And he never spared himself . . . nor did others spare him. And for what purpose . . . why?"

"Yes, a man in a hundred!" came a deep voice from the dining-room.

Olga Ivanovna recalled her life with Duimoff, from beginning to end, in all its details; and suddenly she realised that her husband was indeed an exceptional man, a rare—compared with all her other friends— a great man. And remembering how he was looked up to by her late father and by all his colleagues, she understood that there was indeed good reason to predict for him future fame. The walls, the ceiling, the lamp, the carpet winked at her derisively, as if saying, "You have let it slip by, slip by!" With a cry, she rushed out of the room, slipped past some unknown man in the dining-room, and rushed into her husband's study. Covered with a counter-pane to the waist, Duimoff lay, motionless, on the couch. His face had grown thin, and was a greyish-yellow never seen on the living; his black eyebrows and his kindly smile were all that remained of Duimoff. She felt his chest, his forehead, his hands. His chest was still warm, his forehead and hands were icy. And his half-closed eyes looked not at Olga Ivanovna, but down at the counterpane.

"Duimoff!" she cried loudly. "Duimoff!"

She wished to explain to him that the past was but a mistake; that all was not yet lost; that life might yet be happy and beautiful; that he was a rare, an uncommon, a great man; that she would worship him from this day forth, and pray, and torture herself with holy dread. . . .

"Duimoff!" she cried, tapping his shoulder, refusing to believe that he would never awaken. "Duimoff! Duimoff!"

But in the drawing-room Korosteleff spoke to the maid-servant.

"Don't ask silly questions! Go at once to the church watchman, and get the women's address. They will wash the body, and lay it out, and do all that's wanted."

THE HEAD GARDENER'S TALE

THE HEAD GARDENER'S TALE

THE sale of flowers from the greenhouses on Count N.'s estate was attended by few: I, a neighbouring country gentleman, and a young timber-merchant. While the workmen carried out our handsome purchases and packed them in carts, we sat at the greenhouse door, and talked away on every theme imaginable. Indeed, on that warm April morning, to sit in the garden, hear the birds, and see the flowers, restored to freedom, basking in the sun, was more than delightful.

The packing was superintended by the gardener, Mikhail Karlovitch, a worthy old man, with a fat, clean-shaven face. Mikhail Karlovitch wore a waist-coat of fur, and worked in his shirt-sleeves. He kept silence severely, and listened intently to our conversation, waiting for some one to say something new. We all considered him a German, though as a fact his father was a Swede and his mother Russian, and he professed the orthodox faith. He spoke Russian, Swedish, and German, read much in all three languages, and knew no greater pleasure than to be lent some new book, or talked to, for instance, about Ibsen.

He had his weaknesses, innocent, most of them, enough: he called himself head gardener, though he had no juniors; his expression was always needlessly elated and grave; he tolerated no contradiction, and expected others to listen seriously and attentively.

"That young fellow, there, I may tell you, is a pretty rascal," said my neighbour, pointing to a swarthy, gipsy-like workman who drove a water-cart past. "Only last week he was tried for robbery and acquitted. The jury found him insane, though you can see from his snout he's as healthy as a bull. It seems to have become the fashion in Russia lately to acquit criminals, and explain their crimes by mental abnormality. These acquittals, this general weakness and condonation, will have a bad effect. They demoralise the masses; they blunt the sense of justice. People get used to seeing crime go unpunished. Shakespeare put it aptly when he wrote that 'Virtue itself turns vice, being misapplied.'"

"That's true," consented the timber-merchant. "Murder and incendiarism have increased since these acquittals began. Ask the muzhiks."

The gardener Mikhail Karlovitch turned to us and said—

"Do you know, gentlemen, that I always welcome these acquittals? I feel no fear for the cause of morals and justice when I hear the verdict: Not Guilty. On the contrary, I am delighted. Even when reason tells me that the jurymen have made a mistake, even then I rejoice. I put it to you, gentlemen; if judges and jurymen put more faith in *men*—than in clues, speeches, and articles put in evidence, is not this faith in men a higher thing than all practical considerations? Such faith is accessible only to the few—to those who understand and feel Christ."

"It's a good thought," I said.

"And not a new thought. I remember some time long ago hearing a legend on this theme. And a very fine legend," said the gardener, smiling. "I was told it by my late grandmother, my father's mother, a wonderful old woman! She told it in Swedish: in Russian it's less effective, less classical, so to speak."

We asked him to tell us the story, and forget the rudeness of the Russian language. Flattered and content, he lighted a cigarette, looked angrily at the workmen, and began :—

"To a little town, somewhere, there came an old, solitary, ugly man, by name Thompson—or Wilson— the name doesn't count. His profession was a good one : he cured the sick. He was morose and un-communicative, and spoke only when his work required it. He paid no visits, confined his intercourse to silent bows, and lived as modestly as a hermit. The explanation was that he was a scholar; and in those

N

days scholars were different from ordinary men. They spent their days and nights in meditation, in reading books, and in curing the sick; they looked on everything else as worthless, and had no time to speak needless words. The townspeople understood this thoroughly, and did their best not to waste his time with visits and empty gossip. They rejoiced that God at last had sent them a man who could cure their complaints, and were proud to have among them such a remarkable man.

" ' He knows everything,' they said.

"But that was not enough. They might have added, 'He loves every one.' For in this man's breast beat a good, an angel's heart. He forgot that the townspeople were no kin of his, that they were strangers to him; and he loved them as his children, and for their sake was ready to lay down his own life. He suffered, indeed, from consumption; he coughed; yet when they summoned him to some ailing townsman he forgot his own complaints, sacrificed himself, and, panting, hurried up steep hills. He ignored heat and cold; he despised hunger and thirst. He took no fees, and—stranger than all— when his patients died, he followed their coffins to the grave and wept with their kinsmen.

"Soon he became such a needed part of the town's life that people wondered how they had lived before he came. They were grateful beyond words. Old and young, good and bad, honest and thieves—in one word, all—respected him and knew his worth. The town and neighbourhood had not one man who would do this benefactor a wrong, or even think of such. When he left his house his doors and windows lay open, for he knew that the most abandoned thief would not offend him. Sometimes, following his work of mercy, he crossed hills and forests full of hungry vagabonds. But he felt at ease. Once indeed by night when he returned from a sick-bed he was attacked by robbers in a wood. But when they saw his face they took off their caps respectfully and offered him food. When he said that he was not hungry they gave him a warm cloak and led him safe to town, happy that Fate had sent them a chance to show their gratitude to their benefactor. And, further—you can imagine it—my grandmother added that even horses, cows, and dogs knew him, and showed their joy when they saw him.

"But one fine day this man, whose holiness, it seemed, guarded him from all evil, whom even robbers respected—one fine day this man was found murdered. Bloody, with battered skull, he lay in a ravine, and his pale face expressed amazement. Yes; not fear, but merely surprise was his feeling when he saw his executioner before him. You can imagine the grief of the people of the town and neighbourhood! 'What man,' they asked themselves in despair, 'what

man could possibly kill our friend?' The magistrates who held the inquest and saw the good man's
body came to this conclusion. 'Here,' they said,
'we have all the signs of murder. But as there
exists not on earth a man who would kill our doctor,
this can be no case of murder; and the marks on his
body are a mere accident. It is plain that the doctor
fell into the ravine in the darkness and dashed himself
to death.'

"And this opinion was shared by all the town.
They buried their doctor, and no one thenceforth
spoke of his death as a crime. That a man should
exist so infamous as to kill their friend they refused
to believe. Even infamy has its limits? Is it not so?

"But not long afterwards—you may imagine it—
chance pointed to the murderer. A notorious ne'er-
do-well and evil-liver, who had been more than once in
gaol, was caught in a drink-shop selling for liquor the
doctor's snuff-box and watch. When taxed with the
crime he lost his head and told transparent lies. They
searched his house and found in his bed a blood-
stained shirt and the doctor's lancet, which was set
with gold. What further clues were wanted? He
was put in gaol. The townspeople were horrified,
but they continued to say—

"'Incredible! It is impossible. Be sure there is
no mistake; circumstantial evidence like this often
leads to injustice!'

"On trial the murderer obstinately denied his guilt. Everything told against him, and to find him innocent was as hard as to find this earth black. But the judges seemed to have gone out of their minds; they weighed every item of evidence a dozen times; they looked incredulously at the witnesses, they turned red, and drank water. . . . The trial began at early morning and ended only at night.

"'Prisoner!' began the presiding judge, turning to the murderer. 'The court has found you guilty of the murder of Doctor N., and condemns you . . .'

"He intended to say 'to be hanged till you are dead,' but the paper on which the verdict was written dropped from his hand, he rubbed the sweat from his forehead, and cried out—

"'No! May God visit it on me if I judge unjustly, but I swear that this man is innocent! I will not admit the thought that there is a man on earth who would kill our friend the doctor! There is no man alive who would fall so low!'

"'There is no such man alive!' cried the other judges.

"'There is none!' echoed the crowd in court. 'Release him.'

"So the murderer was dismissed in peace, and not one man censured the judges for injustice. And God, added my grandmother, for such faith in his creatures forgave the townspeople all their sins. For He rejoices to think that man is indeed His image, and grieves when, forgetting their human worth, men judge men as dogs. It may be, the verdict of acquittal caused the townspeople harm; but, on the other hand, reflect on the beneficent influence of this deep faith in men, this faith which never lies dead, which fosters our most generous feelings, and inspires us to love and respect our fellow-men. And that is a great thing."

Mikhail Karlovitch said no more. My neighbour was about to reply, but the old gardener with a gesture indicating that he disliked contradiction returned to the carts, and, with his old grave expression, resumed his work.

OYSTERS

OYSTERS

IT needs no straining of memory to recall the rainy twilight autumn evening when I stood with my father in a crowded Moscow street and felt overtaken by a strange illness. I suffered no pain, but my legs gave way, my head hung helplessly on one side, and words stuck in my throat. I felt that I should soon fall on the pavement and swoon away.

Had I been taken to hospital at the moment, the doctor would have written above my bed the word: "Fames"—a complaint not usually dealt with in medical text-books.

Beside me on the pavement stood my father in a threadbare summer overcoat and a check cap from which projected a piece of white cotton-wool. On his feet were big, clumsy goloshes. The vain man, fearing that people might see that the big goloshes covered neither boots nor stockings, had cased his legs in old gaiters.

This poor, unintelligent man, whom I loved all the more, the more tattered and dirty became his once smart summer overcoat, had come to the capital five

months before to seek work as a clerk. Five months
he had tramped the city, seeking employment; only
to-day for the first time he had screwed up his courage
to beg for alms in the street.

In front of us rose a big, three-storied house with
a blue signboard " Restaurant." My head hung helplessly back, and on one side. Involuntarily I looked
upward at the bright, restaurant windows. Behind
them glimmered human figures. To the right were
an orchestrion, two oleographs, and hanging lamps.
While trying to pierce the obscurity my eyes fell on
a white patch. The patch was motionless; its rect-
angular contour stood out sharply against the universal
background of dark brown. When I strained my eyes
I could see that the patch was a notice on the wall,
and it was plain that something was printed upon it,
but what that something was I could not see.

I must have kept my eyes on the notice at least
half an hour. Its whiteness beckoned to me, and, it
seemed, almost hypnotised my brain. I tried to read
it, and my attempts were fruitless.

But at last the strange sickness entered into its
rights.

The roar of the traffic rose to thunder; in the smell
of the street I could distinguish a thousand smells;
and the restaurant lights and street lamps seemed to
flash like lightning. And I began to make out things
that I could not make out before.

"Oysters," I read on the notice.

A strange word. I had lived in the world already eight years and three months, and had never heard this word. What did it mean? Was it the proprietor's surname? No, for signboards with innkeepers' names hang outside the doors, and not on the walls inside.

"Father, what are oysters?" I asked hoarsely, trying to turn my face towards his.

My father did not hear me. He was looking at the flow of the crowd, and following every passer-by with his eyes. From his face I judged that he dearly longed to speak to the passers, but the fatal, leaden words hung on his trembling lips, and would not tear themselves off. One passer-by he even stopped and touched on the sleeve, but when the man turned to him my father stammered, "I beg your pardon," and fell back in confusion.

"Papa, what does 'oysters' mean?" I repeated.

"It is a kind of animal. . . . It lives in the sea. . . ."

And in a wink I visualised this mysterious animal. Something between a fish and a crab, it must be, I concluded; and as it came from the sea, of course it made up into delightful dishes, hot *bouillabaisse* with fragrant peppercorns and bay leaves, or sour *solianka* with gristle, crab-sauce, or cold with horse-radish. . . . I vividly pictured to myself how this fish is brought from the market, cleaned, and thrust quickly into a pot . . . quickly, quickly, because every one is hungry . . . frightfully hungry. From the restaurant kitchen came the smell of boiled fish and crab soup.

This smell began to tickle my palate and nostrils; I felt it permeating my whole body. The restaurant, my father, the white notice, my sleeve, all exhaled it so strongly that I began to chew. I chewed and swallowed as if my mouth were really full of the strange animal that lives in the sea. . . .

The pleasure was too much for my strength, and to prevent myself falling I caught my father's cuff, and leaned against his wet summer overcoat. My father shuddered. He was cold. . . .

"Father, can you eat oysters on fast days?" I asked.

"You eat them alive . . ." he answered. "They are in shells . . . like tortoises, only in double shells."

The seductive smell suddenly ceased to tickle my nostrils, and the illusion faded. Now I understood!

"How horrible!" I exclaimed. "How hideous!"

So that was the meaning of oysters! However, hideous as they were, my imagination could paint them. I imagined an animal like a frog. The frog sat in the shell, looked out with big, bright eyes, and moved its disgusting jaws. What on earth could be more horrible to a boy who had lived in the world just eight years and three months? Frenchmen, they said, ate frogs. But children—never! And I saw this fish being carried from market in its shell, with claws, bright eyes, and shiny tail. . . . The children all hide themselves, and the cook, blinking squeamishly, takes the animal by the claws, puts it on a dish, and carries it to the dining-room. The grown-ups take it, and eat . . . eat it alive, eyes, teeth, claws. And it hisses, and tries to bite their lips.

I frowned disgustedly. But why did my teeth begin to chew? An animal, disgusting, detestable, frightful, but still I ate it, ate it greedily, fearing to notice its taste and smell. I ate in imagination, and my nerves seemed braced, and my heart beat stronger. . . . One animal was finished, already I saw the bright eyes of a second, a third. . . . I ate these also. At last I ate the table-napkin, the plate, my father's goloshes, the white notice. . . . I ate everything before me, because I felt that only eating would cure my complaint. The oysters glared frightfully from their bright eyes, they made me sick, I shuddered at the thought of them, but I wanted to eat. To eat!

"Give me some oysters! Give me some oysters." The cry burst from my lips, and I stretched out my hands.

"Give me a kopeck, gentlemen!" I heard suddenly my father's dulled, choked voice. "I am ashamed to ask, but, my God, I can bear it no longer!"

"Give me some oysters!" I cried, seizing my father's coat-tails.

"And so you eat oysters! Such a little whipper-snapper!" I heard a voice beside me.

Before me stood two men in silk hats, and looked at me with a laugh.

"Do you mean to say that this little manikin eats oysters? Really! This is too delightful! How does he eat them?"

I remember a strong hand dragged me into the glaring restaurant. In a minute a crowd had gathered, and looked at me with curiosity and amusement. I sat at a table, and ate something slippy, damp, and mouldy. I ate greedily, not chewing, not daring to look, not even knowing what I ate. It seemed to me that if I opened my eyes, I should see at once the bright eyes, the claws, the sharp teeth.

I began to chew something hard. There was a crunching sound.

"Good heavens, he's eating the shells!" laughed the crowd. "Donkey, who ever heard of eating oyster shells?"

After this, I remember only my terrible thirst. I lay on my bed, kept awake by repletion, and by a strange taste in my hot mouth. My father walked up and down the room and gesticulated.

"I have caught cold, I think!" he said. "I feel something queer in my head. . . . As if there is something inside it. . . . But perhaps it is only . . . because I had no food to-day. I have been strange altogether . . . stupid. I saw those gentlemen paying ten roubles for oysters; why didn't I go and ask them for something . . . in loan? I am sure they would have given it."

Towards morning I fell asleep, and dreamed of a frog sitting in a shell and twitching its eyes. At midday thirst awoke me. I sought my father; he still walked up and down the room and gesticulated.

WOMEN

o

WOMEN

IN the village of Riabuzhka, directly opposite the church, stands a two-storied house with stone foundations and an iron roof. In the lower story, with his family, lives the owner, Philip Ivanoff Kamin, nick-named "Diudya"; overhead, in rooms very hot in summer and very cold in winter, lodge passing officials, traders, and country gentlemen. Diudya rents land, keeps a drink-shop on the main road, trades in tar and honey and magpies; and is worth a good eight thousand roubles safely lodged in bank.

Feodor, his elder son, is foreman mechanic at a factory; and, as the peasants say, he is so far up the hill that you can't get near him. Ugly and delicate Sophia, Feodor's wife, lives at home with her father-in-law, cries half the day, and every Sunday drives to hospital for treatment. Hunchbacked Aliosha, Diudya's second son, also lives at home. He lately married Varvara, whom he took to wife out of an impoverished house. Varvara is young, pretty, healthy, and fond of dress. The passing officials and traders let no one bring the samovar and make the beds but Varvara.

One evening in July as the sun set, and the air reeked of hay, hot manure, and new milk, into Diudya's yard came a cart with three men. One, aged about thirty, wore a canvas suit; the boy of seven or eight beside him wore a long black coat with big buttons; the third, a young lad in a red shirt, was the driver.

The driver unhitched the horses and walked them up and down the street; and the man of thirty washed, prayed towards the church, and spreading a fur rug beside the cart, sat down with the boy to supper. He ate slowly and gravely; and Diudya, who had studied many a traveller in his day, found him a capable, serious man, who knew his own worth.

Diudya, capless, and in shirt-sleeves, sat on the steps and waited for the traveller to speak. His patrons usually spent the evening story-telling, and their stories gave him pleasure. His old wife Afanasievna and his daughter-in-law Sophia milked cows in a shed; Varvara, wife of his younger son, sat upstairs at an open window and ate sunflower seeds.

" I suppose this boy is your son ? " asked Diudya.

" My adopted son," answered the traveller. " I took him, orphan, for the saving of my soul."

The pair soon gossiped at ease. The traveller seemed a talkative, eloquent man; and Diudya learned that he was a petty burgher from town, a house-owner, by name Matvei Savvitch, that he was on his way to inspect some gardens which he rented from German colonists, and that the boy's name was Kuzka. It was hot and stifling; no one wished to sleep. When it grew dark, and the sky was dotted with pale stars, Matvei Savvitch began to tell the story of Kuzka. Afanasievna and Sophia stood some way off, and Kuzka loitered at the gate.

"I may say, grandfather, that this story is involved in the extreme," began Matvei Savvitch. "If I were to tell you everything that happened it would last all night. Well! About ten years ago in our street, exactly in a line with us, where now stands the candle factory and oil mill, lived Marya Semionovna Kapluntseff, an old widow with two sons. One of these sons was a tram-conductor; the other, Vasya, a lad of my own age, lived at home with his mother. Old Kapluntseff had kept horses—five pairs of them— and sent his draymen all over town; and his widow continued the business, and, as she managed the draymen no worse than her husband, on some days she made a clear five roubles profit.

"And Vasya, too, had his earnings. He kept prize tumblers and sold them to fanciers; I remember him standing on the roof, throwing up a broom and whistling, and the pigeons would fly right into the sky. He trapped goldfinches and starlings, and made good cages. A trifling business, you think, but you can easily make your ten roubles a month out of trifles.

Well . . . as time passed the old woman lost the use of her legs, and lay all day in bed. The house remained without mistress, and what is that but a man without eyes? The old woman resolved to marry her Vasya. She hired a match-maker, did everything quickly . . . woman's talk . . . and Vasya went to have a look at his bride. She was the widow Samokvalika's Mashenka. Vasya didn't waste time over it; in one week the whole business was finished. She was a young girl, little, shortish, with a white, pleasant face—all the qualities of a young lady; and a portion too, not bad—five hundred roubles, a cow, a bed! And the old woman—she felt it coming—two days after the wedding set out for Jerusalem of the hills, where there is neither sickness nor sighs. The young ones said mass for her soul and began to live. Six months they lived together happily; and then, suddenly, a new misfortune! Vasya was summoned to draw lots as a conscript. They took him, poor fellow, as a soldier, and remitted nothing. They shaved his head, and packed him off to the kingdom of Poland. It was God's will, and there was no appeal. When he said good-bye to his wife in the yard he was cool enough, but, looking upwards at the hayloft with the pigeons, he cried as if his heart would break. It hurt me to see him. For company's sake Mashenka took her mother to live with her; and the mother stayed till child was the born, that is, this same Kuzka; and then went away to another married daughter who lived at Oboyan. So Mashenka was left with her child. And there were five draymen, all drunken and impudent; horses and carts; broken fences and soot catching fire in the chimneys—no affair at all for a woman. And as I was a neighbour, she would come to me on all sorts of business; and I did my best for her, arranged more than one affair, gave her advice. And sometimes I would go to her house, have a drink, and a bit of a chat. I was a young man, clever, and I loved to talk about things; and she, too, was educated and had good manners. She dressed neatly and carried a parasol in summer. I remember; I would start upon theology or politics, and she felt flattered by this, and would treat me to tea and jam. . . . In short, grandfather, I will waste no more words on it, a year had not passed when the unclean spirit seized me, the enemy of all mankind! I noticed that when a day passed without meeting Mashenka I felt out of sorts, and was bored. And all my time was spent in finding excuses to call on her. 'It's time,' I'd say to myself, 'to put in the double window-frames'; and I would spend the whole day in her house putting in the frames, and carefully leaving the work unfinished, so as to return next day. 'We ought to count Vasya's pigeons, and make sure none are lost.' And so on always. I spent hours talking to her across the fence; and at last, to avoid going round to the door, I made a

little gate in the fence. Woman's sex is the cause of
much evil and offence in this world! Not only we,
sinners, but even holy men are seduced. Mashenka
did not repulse me. When she ought to have thought
of her husband, and kept guard on her conduct, she
fell in love with me. I noticed soon that she also was
tired of it, and that she spent all day walking along
the fence and looking through the crevices into my
yard.

"My head whirled round. On Thursday in Holy
Week I was up early, before daybreak; I had to go to
market. I had to pass the gate; and the devil was
there! The grating of the gate was raised, and there
stood Mashenka in the middle of the yard, already up,
and busy feeding the ducks. I lost control of myself.
I called her by name. She came up and looked at me
through the grating. Her face was white, her eyes
were sleepy and caressing. I liked her very much!
And I began to pay her compliments as if we were not
at the gate, but as if it were a birthday visit. And
Mashenka blushed, laughed, and looked at me with the
same eyes, never taking them off me. I went quite
mad, and told her straight that I loved her. She
opened the gate, let me in, and from that day forward
we lived as man and wife."

Matvei paused. Into the yard, breathless, came
hunchback Aliosha, and, without looking at the group,
ran into the house; a minute later he rushed out with

a concertina, and, jingling the coppers in his pocket and chewing a sunflower seed, disappeared behind the gate.

"Who is that man?" asked Matvei Savvitch.

"My son Alexei," answered Diudya. "He's gone off to amuse himself, rascal! God cursed him with a hump, so we're not hard on him!"

"He does nothing but play with the children," sighed Afanasievna. "Before Shrovetide we married him, and thought he'd improve, but he's got worse than ever."

"It was no use," said Diudya. "We only made a strange girl happy, without profit."

From behind the church came the sound of a mournful but pleasant song. The words were indistinguishable, but the voices, two tenors and a bass, could easily be made out. All listened. Suddenly two of the singers, with a loud laugh, ceased to sing, but the third, the tenor, continued, and sang so high that all mechanically looked upward as if they thought the voice had reached the sky. Varvara came out of the house, and, shading her eyes with her hand as if the sun dazzled her, looked at the church.

"It's the priest's sons and the schoolmaster," she said. Again all three voices sang together. Matvei Savvitch sighed and continued:—

"So it happened, grandfather! . . . Well, in two years a letter came from Vasya. He wrote from

Warsaw and told us that he had been discharged for
ill-health. He was invalided. But by that time I
had driven my madness out of my head, and, what's
more, I was thinking of making a good match, and
was only waiting an excuse to get rid of my love-
bird. Every day I resolved to speak to Mashenka,
but I never knew how to begin, and I can't abide
a woman's howl. The letter gave me my chance. As
Mashenka read it aloud to me she turned white as
snow, and I said to her, 'Glory be to God,' I said.
'Thou wilt again be an honest woman.' She answered, 'I will not live with him.' 'But he is your
husband.' 'That is nothing to me,' she answered.
'I never loved him, and I married him against my
will. My mother forced me to.' 'But that doesn't
get round the question, fool,' I said. 'Were you
married to him in church or not?' 'I was married in
church,' she answered me, 'but I love only thee, and
I will be thy wife till thy very death. Let people
jeer at me! I care nothing for them!' 'You are
a believing woman,' I said to her. 'You read the
Bible; what is there written there?'"

"Once given to her husband with her husband she
must live," said Diudya.

"Husband and wife are of one flesh and blood,"
resumed Matvei Savvitch. "'Thou and I have
sinned,' I said. 'We must listen to our consciences and
have the fear of God. We will ask forgiveness of

Vasya. He is a peaceful, timid man—he won't murder you. But better,' I added, ' far better in this world to tolerate torture from thy lawful husband than gnash thy teeth when the Day of Judgment is nigh!' The silly wouldn't listen to me. Not a word would she say but 'I love thee!' and nothing more. Vasya came home on the Saturday before Trinity early in the morning. I watched the whole business through the fence. In ran Vasya into the house, and a minute later out he came with Kuzka in his arms, laughing and crying at the same time. He kissed Kuzka and looked up at the hayloft; he wanted to go to his pigeons, but he wouldn't let hold of Kuzka. He was a soft sort of man—sentimental! The day passed quietly enough. They rang the bells for the vesper service, and I kept thinking to myself, ' Why don't they decorate the gates and the yard with birches? Something is wrong,' I thought. I went into their house and looked. Vasya sat on the floor in the middle of the room, twitching his eyes as if in drink; the tears flowed down his cheeks, his hands shook; he took out of his handkerchief cracknels, necklaces, gingerbread—all sorts of gifts—and threw them on the floor. Kuzka—he was then aged three— crept on the floor and chewed the gingerbreads; and Mashenka stood by the stove, pale and trembling, and muttered, 'I am not thy wife; I will not live with thee,' and a lot more nonsense of that kind.

I threw myself on the boards at Vasya's feet and said, 'We two are guilty before thee, Vassili Maksimuitch; forgive us for the love of Christ!' and then I rose and said to Mashenka, 'It is your duty, Marya Semionovna, to wash Vassili Maksimuitch's feet, and be to him an obedient wife, and pray for me to God that He, the All-Merciful, may forgive me my sin.' I was inspired by a heavenly angel! I spoke edification; spoke with such feeling that I began to cry. And two days later up to me comes Vasya. 'I forgive you,' says he; 'I forgive you, Matiusha, and I forgive my wife; God be with you both. She is a soldier's wife after all, and women are queer things; she is young, it was hard for her to guard herself. She is not the first, and she will not be the last. There is only one thing,' he added. 'I beg you henceforth to live as if there was nothing between us; let nothing be seen, and I,'- he says, 'will try to please her in everything so that she may love me again.' He gave me his hand on it, drank some tea, and went away contented. 'Glory be to God!' I said to myself; and I felt happy that all had been settled so well. But hardly had Vasya got outside the yard when Mashenka appears. I had no peace, you see! She hung on my neck, howled, and implored me 'For the love of God do not forsake me! I cannot live without thee! I cannot, I cannot!'"

"The shameless trull!" sighed Diudya.

"But I bawled at her, stamped my feet, dragged her into the hall, and locked the door. 'Go back!' I shouted, 'to thy husband. Do not shame me before the people! Have the fear of God in thy heart.' And every day this history was repeated. I stood one morning in the yard near the stable and mended a bridle. Suddenly up I looked, and saw her running through the gate, bare-footed, with nothing on but a petticoat. Straight up to me she ran, seized the bridle, and got covered with tar, and trembling all over, howled, 'I cannot live with that brute! It is beyond my strength. If thou no longer lovest me, then kill me!' It was too much for my patience. I struck her twice with the bridle. But at that moment in runs Vasya and cries despairingly, 'Don't strike her, don't strike her!' But he himself seemed to have gone out of his mind, for, flourishing his arms, he began to beat her with his clenched fists with all his might, then flung her down in the dust, and trampled her into it. I tried to defend her, but he seized hold of the reins, and beat her without mercy. Beat her as he'd beat a horse, gee, gee, gee!"

"A good thing if they did it to you," growled Varvara, walking away. "You murdered our sister between you, accursed!"

"Hold your tongue!" shouted Diudya. "Mare!"

"Gee, gee, gee!" continued Matvei Savvitch. "One of the draymen ran in from his yard; I called up some of my workmen, and between us we rescued Mashenka and carried her home. It was a shame! She lay there in bed, all bandaged, all in compresses—only her eyes and nose could be seen—and looked up at the ceiling.

"'Good day, Marya Semionovna,' I would say to her. But she spoke not a word.

"And Vasya sat in another room, tore his hair, and cried, 'I am a ruffian! I have murdered my wife! Send me in Thy mercy, Lord, death!'

"I sat half an hour with Mashenka, and spoke edification. I frightened her.

"'The righteous,' I said. 'The righteous of this world are rewarded in Paradise, but thy place is fiery Gehenna with all adulteresses. . . . Do not dare resist thy husband, go down on thy knees to him!' But she hadn't a word for me; even her eyes were still; I might as well have preached to a pillar.

"A day later Vasya was taken ill—something, it was, like cholera; and that same evening I heard he was dead. They buried him. Mashenka was not at the funeral; she wouldn't let people see her shameless face and her blue marks. But soon they began to say in town that Vasya's death was not natural, that he was murdered by Mashenka. The police soon heard it. They dug up Vasya, cut him open, and found his stomach full of arsenic. It was a simple case. Of course, the police took away Mashenka, and with her nnocent Kuzka. They put her in gaol. . . . About eight months later she was tried. She sat, I remember, in the dock in a grey gown with a white handkerchief on her head—thin, pale, sharp-eyed, the picture of misery. And behind her a soldier with a rifle! Of course she denied it. Some said she'd poisoned her husband; others argued that he had poisoned himself from grief. Anyway, I was a witness. When they questioned me I told them the honest truth. 'She was a sinful woman,' I told them. 'She did not love her husband—it's no use hiding it. She was an obstinate woman. . . .' The trial began in the morning and didn't end till night. It was penal servitude in Siberia, thirteen years of it.

"Mashenka remained in our local gaol three months after trial. I used to go and see her. I was sorry for her, and would bring her tea and sugar. . . . And she—I remember—when she caught sight of me, would wring her hands, and mutter, 'Go away! Go away.' And Kuzka would press himself to her dress, as if he feared I might take him. 'Look!' I would say to Mashenka. 'See what you've brought yourself to! *Akh*, Masha, Masha, perishing soul! When I tried to teach you reason, you wouldn't listen; so weep now! It is you yourself,' I would say, 'who are guilty; accuse yourself!' And I spoke edification to her; but the only words she answered were, 'Go away! Go away!' Then she'd press little Kuzka to the wall, and tremble all over. Well! When she was taken out of our province, I went to see her off at the railway station, and put into her hand a rouble, for Christ's sake. She didn't reach Siberia. Before she had crossed the government frontier she was down with gaol-fever, and in gaol she died."

"To a dog a dog's death!" said Diudya.

"Kuzka was sent back. I thought the matter out, and took him to live with me. What else could I do? He's a sprig of a gaol-bird, that's true, but all the same he's a Christian, a living soul. I was sorry for him. I will make him a clerk, and if I have no children of mine, a trader. Nowadays, wherever I go I take him with me; he is learning business."

While Matvei Savvitch told his story, Kuzka sat on a stone at the gate, and, resting his head on his hands, looked at the sky; when it grew dusk he looked like a stump of a tree.

"Kuzka, go to bed!" cried Matvei Savvitch.

"It's time," said Diudya, rising. He yawned audibly, and added, "They think themselves clever and disobey their elders—that's the cause of their troubles."

The moon already shone in the sky overhead; it seemed to speed swiftly to one side and the clouds beneath it to the other; the clouds drifted away and the moon was soon clear of them. Matvei Savvitch prayed towards the church, bade the others good night, and lay on the ground near his cart. Kuzka also prayed, lay down in the cart, and covered himself with a coat; to increase his comfort he made a hollow in the hay, and bent in two until his elbows touched his knees. From the yard could be seen Diudya, lighting a candle in the lower story; after which he took his spectacles, stood in the corner with a book, bowed before the ikon, and read.

The travellers slept. Afanasievna and Sophia crept up to the cart, and looked at Kuzka.

"The orphan's asleep," said the old woman. "All skin and bone, poor lad! No mother on earth, and no one to feed him on his journey."

"My Grishutka, I think, is about two years older," said Sophia. "He lives in that factory like a slave, and has no mother either. ... His master beats him. When I first looked at this lad he reminded me of my Grishutka; the blood in my heart froze up."

Five minutes passed in silence.

"I wonder does he remember his mother," said the old woman.

"How should he remember?"

And from Sophia's eyes fell big tears.

"He's twisted himself into a roll," she said, sobbing and laughing from pity and emotion. "Poor little orphan!"

Kuzka started and opened his eyes. He saw above him an ugly, wrinkled, tear-stained face; and near it another face, old and toothless, with a sharp chin and

P

a humped nose; and above the faces was the unfathomable sky with its flying clouds and moon. He cried
out with terror. Sophia also cried out; an echo
answered both; and the heavy air seemed to tremble
with restlessness. A watchman not far off signalled:
a dog barked. Matvei Savvitch muttered in his sleep,
and turned on the other side.

Late at night when the others—Diudya, his wife, and
the watchman—were asleep, Sophia came out to the
gate and sat on a bench. The heat was still stifling,
and her head ached from crying. The street was
wide and long; it stretched two versts to the right,
and two more to the left—there was no end to it.
One side only was lighted by the moon; the other lay
in deep gloom; the long shadows from poplars and
starling-cotes stretched across it, and the black and
menacing shadow of the church spread far, embracing
Diudya's gate and half his house. No one moved
or spoke. But from the end of the street came
faint sounds of music. Aliosha played on his concertina.

Something moved in the shadow of the church fence;
but no one could say whether it was man or cow, or
neither—perhaps the sound came from some big bird
rustling in the trees. But suddenly out of this shadow
came a figure, and this figure stopped, said something
in a man's voice, and disappeared down a lane near the
church. A minute later, two fathoms from the gate

emerged a woman, who, seeing Sophia on the bench, stood still.

"Varvara, is it you?" asked Sophia.

"I."

It was Varvara. She stood still a moment longer, then came up to the bench and sat down.

"Where have you been?" asked Sophia.

Varvara was silent.

"You will bring the same end on yourself, young one," said Sophia. "You heard about Mashenka, and the trampling underfoot . . . and the reins. Take care that something of that sort doesn't happen to you."

"I don't care if it does."

Varvara laughed in her handkerchief, and said in a whisper—

"I have been with the priest's son."

"Nonsense?"

"I swear."

"It's a sin!" whispered Sophia.

"I don't care. It's nothing to regret. A sin is a sin, and better the lightning strike me than lead such a life. I am young . . . and healthy, and my husband is a hunchback, miserable, surly, worse than Diudya accursed! Before I was married I had not enough to eat and walked barefoot; but for the sake of Aliosha's money I became a slave, like a fish in a net, and I would sooner sleep with a serpent than with this scabby Aliosha. And your life? Can you bear it? Your Feodor sent you home to his father from the factory, and lives there with another woman; he took your boy away from you and sold you into slavery. You work like a horse, and never hear a decent word. Better never marry, better take half-roubles from the son of the priest, better beg for bread, drown yourself in a well . . ."

" It's a sin ! " sighed Sophia.

" I don't care."

From the church again came the mournful song of the three voices, the two tenors and the bass. And again the words were indistinguishable.

And Varvara began to whisper that she went out at night with the priest's son, and told what he said to her, and what his friends were like; and that she carried on also with passing officials and traders. And Sophia began to laugh; she felt it was sinful and awful and sweet to listen; and she envied Varvara, and felt sorry that she had not been a sinner when she was young and handsome.

The church bells struck midnight.

" It's time for bed," said Sophia, rising. " Diudya may catch us."

Both went cautiously into the yard.

" I went away and didn't hear what happened to Mashenka afterwards," said Varvara, spreading her bed under the window.

"She died, he said, in prison. She poisoned her husband."

Varvara lay down beside Sophia, thought, and said softly—

"I could murder my Aliosha without a qualm."

"You talk nonsense, God be with you."

When Sophia was almost asleep Varvara pressed against her and whispered in her ear—

"Let us murder Diudya and Aliosha!"

Sophia shuddered and said nothing at first. After a moment she opened her eyes and looked steadfastly at the sky.

"People would find out," she said.

"Nobody'll find out. Diudya is old; his time, in any case, has come; and Aliosha, they'll say, killed himself with drink."

Neither of the women slept. Both thought, silently.

"It's cold," said Sophia, beginning to shudder. "I expect it will soon be light. Are you asleep?"

"No. . '. . Pay no attention to what I said to you," whispered Varvara. "I lose my temper with them, accursed, and sometimes don't myself know what I say. . . . Go to sleep!"

The two women were silent, and gradually calmed down and went to sleep.

Old Afanasievna awoke first of all. She called Sophia, and both went to the shed to milk the cows.

Next appeared hunchback Aliosha, hopelessly drunk, and without his concertina. His chest and knees were covered with dust and straw; it was plain he had fallen on the road. Rolling tipsily from side to side, he went into the shed and, without undressing, threw himself on a sledge and at once began to snore. When the rising sun burnt with a fierce glow the crosses on the church, when later the windows imaged it, when across the yard through the dewy grass stretched shadows from the trees, only then did Matvei Savvitch rise and begin to bustle about.

"Kuzka, get up!" he shouted. "It's time to yoke the horses. Look sharp!"

The morning's work began. A young Jewess in a brown, flounced dress led a horse to water. The windlass creaked plaintively, the bucket rattled. Kuzka, sleepy, unrested, covered with dew, sat on the cart and drew on his coat lazily and, listening to the water splashing in the well, shuddered from the cold.

"Auntie!" cried Matvei Savvitch. "Sing out to my lad to come and yoke the horses!"

And at the same minute Diudya called out of the window—

"Sophia, make the Jewess pay a kopeck for the water. They take it always, the scabbies!"

Up and down the street ran bleating sheep; women bawled at the shepherd; and the shepherd played his reed, flourished his whip, and answered in a rough, hoarse bass. Three sheep ran into the yard and crowded together at the fence. The noise awoke Varvara, who took her bed in her arms and went towards the house.

"You might at least drive out the sheep!" cried the old woman. "My fine lady!"

"What more? You think I'll work for a pack of Herods like you," growled Varvara, entering the house.

The axles were soon oiled and the horses harnessed. From the house came Diudya with an abacus, and, sitting on the steps, made up his account against the travellers for lodging, oats, and water.

"You charge high, grandfather, for the oats," said Matvei Savvitch.

"If they're too dear, don't take them. We won't force you to."

When the travellers were ready to climb into the cart an accident delayed them. Kuzka had lost his cap.

"What have you done with it, swine?" bawled Matvei Savvitch angrily. "Where is it gone to?"

Kuzka's face was contorted with terror. He searched about the cart and, finding no cap there, went to the gates. The old woman and Sophia also searched.

"I'll cut off your ears," roared Matvei Savvitch. "Accursed pup!"

The cap was found at the bottom of the cart. Kuzka brushed the hay from it, put it on timidly as if he expected a blow from behind, and took his seat. Matvei Savvitch crossed himself, the driver pulled the reins, and the cart rolled slowly out of the yard.

WOE

WOE

THE turner, Grigori Petroff, long reputed the cleverest craftsman and most shiftless muzhik in all Galtchink canton, drove his old woman to the Zemstvo hospital. It was a good thirty versts, on an impossible road, a road too bad for the driver of the mail-car, much less for ne'er-do-well turner Grigori. In the turner's face beat a sharp, icy wind; around whirled white snow-clouds, and it was hard to say whether the snow came from heaven or from earth. The snow concealed fields, telegraph posts, and trees; and when the strongest gusts blew in Grigori's face, he could hardly see the yoke. The exhausted mare barely tottered along. All its strength seemed spent in dragging its hoofs out of the deep snow, and shaking its head. The turner was in a hurry. He fidgeted restlessly on his seat, and occasionally whipped his mare.

"Don't cry, Matrena!" he stammered. "Bear it a little longer! We'll soon, God grant, be at the hospital, and then you'll . . . Pavl Ivanuitch'll give you a powder, or let your blood; perhaps he'll rub some sort of spirit into you. Pavl Ivanuitch

will do his best. . . . He'll shout, and stamp his feet,
but he'll do his best. . . . He's a first-rate doctor, he
knows his business, may God be good to him! . . .
The minute we arrive he'll run out of his lodgings
and look at you. 'What!' he'll shout at me. 'Why
didn't you come before? Do you think I am a dog
to waste all day with you devils? Why didn't you
come in the morning? Begone! Come back to-
morrow!' And I will answer, 'Mister doctor! Pavl
Ivanuitch! Your honour! . . .'"

The turner whipped his horse, and without looking
at his old woman, continued to mutter—

"'Your honour! Truly before God! . . . on my
oath, I started at daybreak. . . . How could I get
here sooner when God . . . the Mother of God was
angry and sent such a storm? You can see for yourself! Even with a good horse I couldn't get here in
time, and, as you can see for yourself, mine is not a
horse, but a disgrace!' And Pavl Ivanuitch will frown
and shout, 'I know you! Always the same excuse!
You, in particular, Grisha! I've known you for years.
You stopped five times at a drink-shop!' And I shall
answer him, 'Your honour! Don't think me a
ruffian! My old woman is giving her soul to God;
she's dying! Do you think I'd go near a drink-shop?
May they be cursed, these drink-shops!' Then Pavl
Ivanuitch will tell them to take you into the hospital.
And I shall bow to the ground. 'Pavl Ivanuitch!

Your honour! I thank you humbly! Forgive us —
fools, anathemas; don't condemn us, poor muzhiks!
You ought to kick us out of the hall! Yet you come
out to meet us, and wet your legs in the snow!'

"And Pavl Ivanuitch will look as if he wanted to
hit me, and say, 'Don't throw yourself at my feet,
fool! You'd do better to drink less vodka and have
pity on your wife. You ought to be flogged!' 'That's
God's truth, Pavl Ivanuitch, may I be flogged; may
God flog me! But why not throw myself at your
feet? You are our benefactor, our own father! Your
honour! It is the truth, before God; spit in my face
if I lie: as soon as my Matrena, this same Matrena,
gets well, I will make anything your honour wants.
A cigar-case, if you wish it, of yellow birch . . . a set
of croquet balls, nine-pins—I can make them like
the best foreign ones. . . . I will make them all for
you. I won't charge a kopeck. In Moscow such cigar-
cases cost four roubles. I won't take a kopeck.' And
the doctor will laugh and say to me, 'Well, well . . .
agreed! I'm sorry for you. Only it's a pity you're
such a drunkard!' I know how to manage with these
gentlemen! There's no man on earth I can't stand up
to. Only may God keep us from losing the road!
Akh, my eyes are full of snow."

And the turner muttered without cease. As if to
dull the pain of his own feelings, he babbled on
mechanically. But many as the words on his lips, there

were still more thoughts and problems in his head. Woe
had come upon the turner suddenly, unexpectedly ; and
now he could not recover his self-possession. Till now
he had lived peacefully in drunken apathy, insensible
to sorrow and to joy ; and now he had been struck an
intolerable blow. The shiftless, drunken lie-abed
suddenly found himself busy, tormented, and, it seemed,
in conflict with Nature herself.

The turner remembered that his sorrows began only
yesterday. When, drunk as usual, he had returned
to his home the night before, and, by virtue of old
custom, abused his wife and shook his fists at her, the
old woman looked at him as she had never looked
before. Formerly her old eyes expressed martyrdom,
and the affection of a much-beaten, badly-fed dog ;
this night she looked at him morosely, steadfastly, as
only saints and dying women look. With these
unaccustomed eyes, all the trouble began. The frightened turner borrowed a neighbour's horse, and was
driving the old woman to hospital in the hope that
Pavl Ivanuitch with powders and ointments would
restore to his wife her old expression.

"And listen, Matrena," he stammered. "If Pavl
Ivanuitch asks do I ever beat you, say no, never! For
I will never beat you again! I swear it. I never did
beat you out of anger. I beat you only casually! I
am sorry for you now. Another man would pay no
attention to you, but I take you to hospital. . . . I

do my best. But the storm, the storm, Lord God, Thy will! May God keep us from losing the road! Does your side hurt? Matrena, why don't you answer? I ask, does your side hurt?

"Why is it the snow doesn't melt on her face?" he asked himself, feeling a cold wind on his back and frozen legs. "My snow thaws, but hers. . . . It's strange!"

He could not understand why the snow on his wife's face did not thaw, why her face was drawn-out, severe, and serious, and had turned the colour of dirty wax.

"You are a fool!" muttered the turner. "I spoke to you from my conscience, before God! . . . and you haven't the manners to answer. . . . Fool! If you're not more careful, I won't take you to Pavl Ivanuitch!"

The turner dropped the reins, and thought. He could not make up his mind to look at his wife. He was nervous; and soon his wife's unmannerly silence frightened him. At last, to end his uncertainty, without looking at his wife, he felt her icy hand. The uplifted hand fell, as a whip.

"She's dead, I suppose. An adventure!"

And the turner wept. He wept less from grief than vexation. He reflected how quickly everything happens in this world; how he had hardly entered into his woe ere the woe was past. He hardly seemed to have had time to live with his wife, speak to her, feel for her, and now she was dead. True, they had lived together forty years, but the forty years had fled away like a mist. What with drink, poverty, and quarrels, life had passed away unlived. And, what was bitterest of all, the old woman died at a moment when he felt that he pitied her, could not live without her, and was guilty before her.

"And she even went out and begged," he remembered. "I sent her myself to beg bread. An adventure! She ought to have lived another ten years. She thought, I suppose, that I'm really a bad lot. Mother in heaven, where am I driving to? It's no more a case of cure, but of funerals. Turn back."

The turner turned back and flogged his horse with all his might. The road grew worse and worse. He could no longer see even the yoke. Sometimes the sledge drove into young fir-trees, sometimes something dark scratched the turner's hands and flashed past his eyes. But he saw nothing except a whirling field of white.

"To live over again!" he said to himself. He remembered that forty years ago Matrena was young, pretty, and gay, and that she came from a prosperous home. It was his reputation as craftsman that won her. And, indeed, he had every qualification for living well. But soon after marriage he began to drink, he sprawled all day on the stove, and, it seemed to him, he had slept ever since. He remembered his wedding-day, but of what followed he could recall nothing save that he drank, sprawled, fought. And so passed forty years.

The white snow-clouds turned slowly grey, Evening was near.

"Where am I going?" asked the turner. "I ought to be taking her home, and here I am still going to hospital! I am going crazy!"

The turner again pulled round his horse and again flogged it. The mare strained all her strength, snorted, and broke into a trot. Behind the turner something tapped, tapped, tapped; and though he dared not look around, he knew that it was his wife's head banging against the back of the sledge. As the air darkened the wind blew colder and sharper.

"To live over again!" thought the turner. "To get new tools, to take orders, to give money to the old woman. . . . Yes!"

He dropped the reins. A moment later he tried to find them, but failed. His hands no longer obeyed him.

"It is all the same," he thought. "She will go on herself. She knows the road. To sleep a bit now. . . . Then the funeral, a mass. . . ."

He closed his eyes and slumbered. A moment later, as it seemed to him, the horse stopped. He opened his eyes and saw before something dark, a cabin or hayrick.

He tried to get out of the sledge to find out where

Q

he was, but his body was numbed with such pleasant indolence that he felt he would sooner freeze than move. And he fell restfully asleep.

He awoke in a big room with red walls. Through the window came bright sun-rays. The turner saw men before him, and he obeyed his first instinct to show himself off as a serious man, a man with ideas.

"Have a mass served, brothers!" he began. "Tell the priest . . ."

"That is all right!" came back voices. "Lie down!"

"*Batiushka!* Pavl Ivanuitch!" said the turner in amazement. He saw the doctor before him. "Your honour! Benefactor!"

He wished to jump up and throw himself at the doctor's feet. But his hands and feet no longer obeyed him.

"Your honour, where are my legs? Where are my hands?"

"Good-bye to your legs and hands! They're frozen off, that's all. Well, well . . . there's no use crying. You are old . . . glory be to God . . . sixty years' life is enough!"

"Forgive me, your honour! If you could give me five or six years!"

"Why do you want them?"

"The horse isn't mine. I must return it! . . . The old woman must be buried. . . . *Akh*, how quickly things happen in this world! Your honour! Pavl Ivanuitch! A cigar-case of birchwood of the first quality! I will make you croquet-balls . . ."

The doctor waved his hand and went out of the room.

The turner was dead.

ZINOTCHKA

ZINOTCHKA

ON beds of new-mown hay in a peasant's cabin a party of sportsmen settled down for the night. The moon looked through the window; outside, a concertina moaned plaintively. The hay exhaled a heavy, irritating smell. The sportsmen spoke of dogs, of women, of first love, of snipe. When they had picked to pieces all the women they knew and told a hundred stories, the stoutest of the party, who looked in the darkness like a haycock and spoke in the thick voice of a staff-officer, yawned audibly and remarked—

"There is nothing so wonderful, after all, in being loved; women exist only for that—to love our brother. But tell me, can any of you boast that he has been really hated—hated passionately, hated as devils hate? Has any one ever witnessed an ecstasy of detestation? Eh?"

There was no answer.

"I fancy not," resumed the staff-officer's bass. "I alone have had that experience. I have been hated by a girl, and a pretty girl; and, in my own person, studied all the symptoms of first hate. I say 'first,' gentlemen, because it was the converse of first love. But, as a fact, I gained my queer experience at an age when I had no definite ideas about either love or hatred. I was only eight years old. But that is not the point; the girl herself is the centre of the story. However. . . . Listen!

"One fine summer evening before sunset, with my governess Zinotchka, an entrancing, romantic creature just out of school, I sat in the nursery at lessons. Zinotchka looked abstractedly out of the window and said to me—

"'Yes, we inhale oxygen. Now tell me, Petya, what do we exhale?'

"'Carbonic acid gas,' I answered, also looking out of the window.

"'Quite right,' said Zinotchka. 'The plants, on the other hand, inhale carbonic acid and exhale oxygen. Carbonic acid gas is contained in seltzer water and in samovar smoke. . . . It is a very dangerous gas. Near Naples there is a so-called Dog's Cavern full of it; if you put a dog in this cavern it is quickly suffocated.'

"This unhappy cavern near Naples was a physical phenomenon which no governess ever forgot. Zinotchka always impressed on me strongly the value of natural science, though she knew nothing about chemistry save the fate of these dogs.

"She told me to repeat the facts. I repeated them; whereupon she asked me, 'What is the horizon?' I answered. While we were busy with the horizon my father was in the yard preparing a shooting excursion. The dogs whined, the horses paced impatiently; the servants filled the tarantass with bags of food—all sorts of good things! Alongside the tarantass waited our two-seated droschky, which was to take my mother and sisters on a birthday visit to Ivanitsky's. All were going somewhere, except myself, and my elder brother, who complained of a bad toothache. You can imagine my envy and boredom.

"'So . . . what is it we inhale?' asked Zinotchka, looking out of the window.

"'Oxygen.'

"'Yes; and the horizon is the place where, as it seems to us, the earth is joined to the sky.'

"But at this point the tarantass drove away, and after it the droschky. I looked at Zinotchka and saw that she took from her pocket a piece of paper, crushed it nervously, and pressed it to her forehead. When she had done this she started and looked at the clock.

"'So . . . remember,' she resumed. 'Near Naples there is a so-called Dog's Cavern . . .'—here she again looked at the clock and continued—'where, as it seems to us, the earth is joined to the sky.'

"Poor Zinotchka walked up and down the room in

intense agitation and continued to look at the clock. But my lessons were due to last another half-hour.

"'Take your arithmetic,' she said, breathing heavily, and turning over the pages with a trembling hand. 'Try and solve Problem No. 325. I shall be back immediately.'

"Zinotchka left the room. I heard her fluttering down the stairs, and soon saw through the window her blue dress flashing through the yard and vanishing at the garden gate. Her feverish movements, the redness of her cheeks, her intense agitation aroused my curiosity. Where had she run to, and why? Being intelligent beyond my years, I reasoned it out and understood everything. Taking advantage of my rigid parents' absence, she had gone to plunder the raspberry bushes or, perhaps, to pick wild cherries. If that was so, then I, too, devil take me! would go and pick wild cherries. I threw my lesson-book away and ran into the garden. At the cherry-trees, which I made for first, Zinotchka was not to be seen. Having ignored the raspberries, the gooseberries, and passed our watchman's hut, she was making her way to the pond, pale as death, and starting at every sound. I stole after her, undiscovered, and saw, gentlemen, a most amazing sight! Near the pond, between the trunks of two old willows, stood my elder brother Sasha without the least sign of toothache about him. He looked at approaching Zinotchka, and his whole face, like the sun, was lighted with rapturous delight. And Zinotchka, as if she were being driven into the Dog's Cavern to inhale carbonic acid gas, walked towards him slowly, breathing with difficulty, and hanging back her head. Everything showed that this was the first such meeting of her life. In a moment she stood before my brother, and for a few seconds they looked silently at one another as if they could not credit their own eyes. . . . And then some inexplicable force seemed to push Zinotchka from behind; she laid her hand on Sasha's shoulder and pressed her head against his waistcoat. My brave Sasha smiled, muttered something inaudible, and with the awkwardness of a man very much in love put both his hands to Zinotchka's face. And then, gentlemen, wonders! . . . The hill behind which the sun was sinking, the two willow-trees, the green banks, the sky—all of these were imaged in the pond. Silence . . . you can imagine it! Over the sedges swept a million gold butterflies with long whiskers, beyond the garden a shepherd drove his flock! It was a picture for the gods!

"But of all that I saw, I understood only one thing. Sasha was kissing Zinotchka! It was improper! If mother knew. They would hear more of it. With a feeling of shame I returned to the nursery, and witnessed no more of the tryst. Being intelligent beyond my years, I bent over my lesson-books, thought, and reasoned it out. And my face grew radiant with a smile of victory. On the one hand, it was profitable to possess another's secret ; on the other, it was flattering that persons in authority, like Sasha and Zinotchka, had been detected in ignorance of the social proprieties. Now they had fallen into my power; and their peace henceforth depended only on my generosity. They would know that soon !

" When bedtime came, Zinotchka as usual came to the nursery to make sure that I had said my prayers and had not got into bed in my clothes. I looked at her pretty, radiant face, and grinned. The secret rent me asunder, and demanded an outlet. I began with hints, and revelled in the effect.

" ' Aha, I know ! ' I began. ' Aha ! '

" ' What do you know ? '

" ' Aha ! I saw you kissing Sasha behind the willows. I went after you, and watched ! '

" Zinotchka started and turned a fiery red. Struck dumb by my words, she dropped into a chair on which were a glass of water and a candlestick.

" ' I saw you and Sasha . . . kissing . . .' I repeated, hopping, and enjoying her confusion. ' Aha ! Wait till I tell mother.'

" At first Zinotchka looked at me earnestly and in terror. Then, convinced that I really did know everything, she seized my hand despairingly, and whispered tremulously—

"'Petya, that is mean. . . . I implore you! For the love of God! be a man . . . don't say anything. . . . Honest boys do not spy. It is mean. I implore you!'

"Poor Zinotchka feared my mother as fire; my mother was a virtuous and high-principled lady. That was one reason for her fright. The second, no doubt, was that my grinning snout seemed a profanation of her first, pure, romantic love. You can imagine her feelings! Through my fault, she must have lain awake all night, for she appeared at breakfast next morning with dark blue circles round her eyes. . . . When after breakfast I came across Sasha I could not curb the temptation to grin and boast.

"'Aha! I know. I saw you kissing Mademoiselle Zina!'

"Sasha looked at me and said—

"'You are an idiot!'

"He was harder to frighten than Zinotchka, and the blow failed. That disappointed me. That Sasha was so bold was proof that he didn't believe I had seen the kiss. But, wait, I consoled myself; I could prove it. At lessons that morning Zinotchka kept her eyes turned away, and stammered constantly.

"She showed no fear; but tried to placate me, gave me full marks for everything, and never once complained to my father of my tricks. Being intelligent beyond my years, I exploited her secret to my profit;

I learned no lessons, entered the class-room walking on my hands, and was grossly impertinent—in short, if I had continued in the same spirit to this day, I should be an expert black-mailer. But only a week passed. The secret irritated and tormented me—it was a splinter in my soul. Heedless of results, I could no longer combat the impulse to let it out, and enjoy the effect. One day at dinner when there were many visitors I grinned sheepishly, looked cunningly at Zinotchka, and began—

"'Aha! I know. . . . I saw . . .'

"'What did you see?' asked my mother.

" Again I looked cunningly at Zinotchka, and then Sasha. You should have seen how Zinotchka flared up, and Sasha's ferocious eyes! I bit my tongue and said no more. Zinotchka turned slowly pale, ground her teeth, and ate nothing. During preparation, that evening, I noticed that a sudden change had come over Zinotchka. Her face was severer, colder, marble-like; and her eyes had a strange expression. I give you my word that even in dogs when they tear to pieces a wolf I have never seen such devouring, annihilating eyes. I was soon to learn what the expression meant. In the midst of a lesson Zinotchka ground her teeth and hissed in my face—

"'I detest you! If you only knew, wretch, disgusting animal, how I hate you; how I hate your cropped head, your infamous ass's ears!'

"But she took fright immediately and continued—

"'I did not mean that for you. I was only repeating a part from a play. . . .'

"After that, gentlemen, she came to my bed every night and looked me steadfastly in the face. She hated me passionately. Yet she could not live without me. It somehow seemed a need for her to watch my detestable face. And then I remember one delightful summer evening. There was a smell of hay, stillness, and so on. The moon shone. I was walking down a garden path, thinking of cherry jam. Suddenly up to me came pale and pretty Zinotchka, seized my arm, and, panting, avowed her feelings.

"'Oh, how I hate you! I have never wished any one such evil as I wish you! I want you to understand that!'

"You can imagine it! The moon, the pale face exhaling passion, the stillness! And, little pig that I was, I revelled in it. I listened to Zinotchka, looked at her eyes. . . . At first it was delightful, because it was new. But in a moment I was overtaken by terror; I screamed loudly, and ran into the house.

"I decided that the only thing was to complain to my mother. And I complained, and told her how I had seen Sasha and Zinotchka kissing. I was an idiot, and did not foresee the result; otherwise I should have held my tongue. . . . When my mother heard me she flamed with indignation, and said—

"'It is not your business to talk of such things. . . . You are too young. But what an example to children!'

"My mother was not only virtuous, she was tactful too. She did her best to avoid a scandal; and rid herself of Zinotchka not at once, but gradually, systematically, as people rid themselves of respectable but tiresome visitors. I remember that when Zinotchka drove away her last glance was directed to the window at which I sat, and I assure you that to this day I remember that look.

"Not long afterwards Zinotchka was my brother's wife. That is the Zinaida Nikolaievna whom you all know. I never met her again until I was a junker. It was hard for her to recognise in the moustached officer the detested Petya—still, her manner to me was not quite that of a relative. . . . And even to-day, despite my good-humoured bald head, my peaceful figure, and meek looks, Zinotchka always looks at me a little askance, and seems out of sorts when I visit my brother. . . . It is plain that first hate is not as quickly forgotten as first love. . . . By Jove! The cocks are crowing already. Good night!"

THE PRINCESS

R

THE PRINCESS

THROUGH the wide, the so-called "Red" gates of the monastery of N. came a *calèche* drawn by four well-fed, well-bred horses. While it was still far away the senior monks and lay brethren, grouped near the nobles' half of the monastery inn, guessed from the coachman and horses that the visitor was their well-known princess, Vera Gavriilovna.

An aged footman jumped down from the box and helped the princess to alight. The princess raised her dark veil, came up to the senior monks to receive their blessing, nodded kindly to the lay brethren, and went to her rooms.

"Well, were you longing to see your princess?" she said to the monks who carried her luggage. "It's a whole month since I've been here. But here I am, at last! . . . And where is the Father Archimandrite? Heavens, I burn with impatience! Wonderful, wonderful old man! You should be proud to have such an Archimandrite!"

When the Archimandrite appeared, the princess exclaimed joyfully, crossed her arms on her breast, and bent her head for his blessing.

" No, no! Let me kiss it!" she cried, seizing his hand and kissing it greedily thrice. " How glad, how glad I am, holy father, to see you at last! You, of course, have forgotten your princess; but I have all along been living my real life in this delightful monastery. How charming everything! Do you know, in this life for God, far from the world's vanities, there is a peculiar charm, holy father, a charm which I feel with my whole soul, but cannot express in words!"

The princess's cheeks grew red and tears came into her eyes. She spoke with passion and without pausing, and the seventy-year-old Archimandrite, serious, ugly, and bashful, kept silence, or interjected abruptly, as a soldier—

"Exactly so, your Excellency . . . I hear . . . I understand. . . ."

"How long will you honour us by staying?" he asked at last.

" Only to-night. In the morning I must drive over to Claudia Nikolaievna—we haven't met for ages. But after to-morrow I shall return, and stay three or four days. I want to rest my soul with you, holy father."

The princess liked to stay in the monastery of N. Within the last two years she had come to love it so dearly that she drove over nearly every summer month, staying sometimes two days, sometimes three, sometimes all the week. The timid lay brethren, the silence, the low ceilings, the smell of cypress, the modest food, the cheap window curtains—all these touched her, awakened joyful emotions, and inclined her to meditation and kindly thoughts. Hardly had she been in her rooms half an hour before it seemed that she, too, had grown timid and modest, and that she smelt of cypress; the past dwindled away and lost its meaning; and the princess began to feel that despite her twenty-nine years, she was very like the old Archimandrite, and had been born, as he, not for wealth and worldly greatness, but for a silent life, veiled from the world outside, a life of twilight, twilight as the rooms. . . .

So it is. Into the dark cell of an ascetic lost in prayer breaks some unexpected sun-ray; a bird perches near the window and sings its song: the grim ascetic cannot but smile, and in his heart, under the heavy burden of remorse, as from under a stone, springs a fountain of quiet, sinless joy. The princess felt that she brought hither some such consolation as the sun-ray, or the bird. Her happy, affable smile, her kindly looks, her voice, her humour, her figure—little, graceful, dressed in simple black—these must indeed awaken in these simple, severe people feelings of emotion and charm. "God has sent us an angel!" must be the thought of the monks. And, feeling that this must indeed be the thought of all, she smiled still more kindly, and tried to look like a bird.

Having taken tea and rested, the princess went for

a walk. The sun had set. The monastery garden breathed to the princess moist odours of newly watered mignonette; the even chanting of the monks borne from the chapel was pleasant, yet sad. The vesper service had begun. The dark windows with little hospitable lamps, the shadows, the old monk with the mug seated in the porch near the image—all expressed such deep, unrebelling restfulness that the princess, somehow, felt that she wanted to cry.

And outside the gates, on the path between wall and birches, evening had already fallen. The air darkened swiftly, swiftly. The princess walked down the path, sat on a bench, and thought.

She thought how good it would be to settle for life in this monastery, where all was silent and resigned as the summer night; to forget for ever her ingrate, dissolute prince, her great estates, the creditors who troubled her every day, her misfortunes, her maid Dasha, on whose face she had only that morning seen an impudent grin. How good it would be to sit out life on this bench and peer between birch-trunks into the valley where the evening mist wandered in patches about; and far, far overhead, in a black, veil-like cloud, rooks flew home to their nests; to watch the two lay brethren, one on a piebald horse, the other on foot, who drove in the horses for the night, both enjoying freedom and playing like little children— their young voices rang loudly through the motionless air, and she could hear every word. How good to sit alone and lend ear to the stillness; now a breeze blew and shook the tree-tops; now a frog rustled in last year's grass; now, beyond the wall, a clock struck the quarters. To sit here, motionless; to listen; to think, to think, to think.

An old woman with a wallet passed down the path. The princess thought that she would stop this old woman and say something kindly, something helpful, and from the heart. But the woman did not look round, and disappeared at a turn in the path.

A little later a tall, grey-bearded man, in a straw hat, came down the path. When he reached the princess he took off his hat and bowed, and from the bald forehead and sharp, humped nose the princess saw that it was Doctor Mikhail Ivanovitch, five years ago her employé at Dubovki. She remembered hearing that this doctor's wife had died a year before, and she wished to show her sympathy and to console him.

"Doctor, you did not recognise me, I think?" she said, smiling kindly.

"Yes, princess, I did," he answered. He raised his hat again.

"Thanks; I thought you had forgotten your princess. People remember only their enemies; they forget their friends. You came to pray!"

"I stay here every Saturday night—professionally, I am the monastery doctor."

" And how are you?" asked the princess, with a sigh. "I heard that you lost your wife. How sad!"

" Yes, princess; it was very sad for me."

" What can we do? We must bear our sufferings meekly. Without God's will not one hair falls from a man's head."

" Yes, princess."

The princess's sighs and kindly, affable smile were met by the doctor coldly and drily. And his expression was cold and dry.

" What shall I say to him?" thought the princess.

" What ages since we last met!" she said at last. " Five whole years! How much has happened, what changes have taken place—it frightens me to think of them! You know that I'm married . . . from a countess become a princess. And that I've already managed to part from my husband. . . ."

" Yes, I heard."

" God sent me many trials. You have no doubt heard, too, that I am nearly ruined. To pay my unhappy husband's debts they sold Dubovki and Kiriakovo and Sophino. I have kept only Baranovo and Mikhailtsevo. It frightens me to look back; how many changes; how many misfortunes; how many mistakes!"

" Yes, princess, the mistakes were many."

The princess reddened. She knew her mistakes; they were so intimate that she only could think and

speak of them. But, unable to restrain herself, she
asked—

"Of what mistakes do you speak?"

"You mentioned them yourself, therefore you must
know." The doctor spoke with a laugh. "Why
dwell on them?"

"No; tell me, doctor. I shall be grateful. And,
please, no ceremony; I love to hear the truth."

"I am not your judge, princess."

"Not my judge? But from your tone it's certain
you know something. What is it?"

"If you insist, I'll tell you. But I am a bad hand
at explaining myself, and may be misunderstood. . . ."

The doctor thought a moment, and began—

"There were many mistakes, but the greatest, in
my opinion, was the general spirit which . . . reigned
on all your estates. You see, I cannot express
myself. What I want to say is that it was not love,
but aversion to men which showed itself in everything.
On this aversion was built your whole life system—
aversion to human voices, to faces, to heads, to steps
. . . in one word, to all that constitutes a man. At
your doors and staircases stood overfed, insolent, idle
lackeys whose business it was to keep out any one
badly dressed; in your hall were high-backed chairs
so that the footmen at your balls and receptions
should not stain the walls with the backs of their
heads; the rooms had thick carpets to deaden human

footsteps; every one who entered was warned to speak as softly and as little as possible, and that he should say nothing which might affect unpleasantly the imagination or nerves. And in your own room you gave no man your hand or asked him to sit, just as now you have neither given me your hand nor asked me to sit . . ."

"Please sit down if you will," said the princess, extending her hand, with a smile. "You should not be angry over such trifles."

"But am I angry?" laughed the doctor. He took off his hat, waved it, and continued hotly. "I tell you frankly I have long been waiting a chance to tell you everything—everything. . . . That is, I want to say that you look on your fellow-creatures much as Napoleon, who regarded them as food for cannon, with this difference: that Napoleon at least had ideas, but you—except aversion—have nothing."

"I have aversion to men?" smiled the princess, shrugging her shoulders in surprise. "I?"

"Yes; you! You want facts? Listen! In Mik-hailtsevo living on alms are three of your former cooks, who lost their sight in your kitchens from the heat. Every one healthy, strong, and handsome on your tens of thousands of acres is taken by you or your friends as footman, lackey, coachman. All these two-legged creatures are brought up in . . . lackeyism, overfed, coarsened, robbed of the image of God. . . . Young doctors, agriculturists, teachers, intelligent workmen of all kinds, my God, are torn from work, from honest toil, and bribed with a bit of bread to play in various dolls' comedies which would make any decent man blush! No young man can serve with you three years without turning into a hypocrite, a flatterer, an informer. . . . Is that right? Your Polish stewards, those base spies, all these Gaetans and Casimirs who gallop from morning to night over your tens of thousands of acres, and for your benefit alone suck blood out of every stone! . . . Excuse me for speaking incoherently, but that doesn't matter. The common people, in your opinion, are not human beings. Yes, and the princes, counts, and bishops who visit you, you look on as decorations and not as living men. But the chief thing . . . the thing that angers me most of all, is that you have property worth a million, yet do for your fellow-creatures nothing!"

Surprised, frightened, offended, the princess sat still. She was at a loss what to say or do. Never before had she been spoken to in that tone. The doctor's unpleasant, angry voice, his awkward, stammering words, hammered in her ears; and it seemed from his gesticulations that he would strike her in the face with his hat.

"That is untrue!" she said gently and appealingly. "I have done much good to people, and you yourself know it."

"Delightful!" cried the doctor. "So you mean to say you regard your charitable work seriously, as something useful, not as a dolls' comedy? It was a comedy from beginning to end, a farce of love-my-neighbour, a farce so transparent that even children and stupid muzhik-women saw through it. Take your—what do you call it?—your hospital for homeless old women, in which you forced me to play the rôle of chief physician while you yourself played the rôle of patroness! O Lord our God, what a comical institution! You built a house with parquet floors, set a weathercock on the roof, and collected ten old village women, and set them to sleep under frieze counterpanes, between sheets of Dutch linen, and eat sugar-candy!"

The doctor laughed loudly into his hat, and stammered quickly—

"A comedy! The servants kept the sheets and counterpanes under lock and key to prevent the old women soiling them—let them sleep, old devil's pepper-castors, on the floor! And the old women daren't sit on their beds, or wear their jackets, or walk on the polished floor! All was kept for show, and hidden away as if the women were thieves; and the old women were fed and clothed secretly by charity, and day and night prayed to God to save them from prison, from the soul-saving exhortations of the well-fed rascals whom you commissioned to look after them. And the higher authorities, what did they do? It's too de-

lightful for words. On two evenings a week up there
galloped thirty-five thousand couriers to announce that
to-morrow the princess—that is you—would visit the
home. Which meant that to-morrow I must neglect
my patients, dress myself up, and go on parade. Very
well! I would arrive. The old women would sit in a
row in clean, new dresses and wait. Near them would
walk that retired garrison rat—the inspector—with his
sugary, informer's grin. The old women would yawn
and look at one another, afraid even to grumble! And
we would all wait. Then up gallops the under-steward,
half an hour later the senior steward, then the factor,
then some one else, and yet another . . . gallopers without end! And all with the same severe, ceremonial
faces! We would wait and wait, stand on one leg,
then on the other, look at our watches—all this, of
course, in dead silence, for we all hated one another.
A whole hour would pass, then another hour, at last a
calèche would appear far off, and . . . and . . ."

The doctor laughed dryly, and continued in a thin
tenor—

"Down you'd get from your carriage; and the old
witches, at a signal from the garrison rat, would sing,
'How glorious is our Lord in Zion, The tongue cannot
express . . .' It was too delightful!"

The doctor laughed in a bass note, and waved his
arm to imply that amusement forbade him to continue.
His laugh was hard and heavy as the laugh of a bad

man, and his teeth ground together. His voice, his face, his glittering, somewhat impudent eyes, showed how deeply he despised the princess, her home, and the old women. In what he had said so awkwardly and rudely, there was nothing really laughable, but he laughed with content, even with pleasure.

"And the school?" he resumed, out of breath with laughter. "Do you remember your attempt to teach the muzhiks' children? You must have taught them nicely, for soon all the boys ran away, and had to be flogged and bribed to go back to your school. And remember how you tried to feed unweaned children out of bottles—with your own hands!—while their mothers worked in the fields! You wandered about the village weeping that there were no children to be had—their mothers had taken them with them to the fields. And then the headman ordered them to leave their children behind for your amusement! Too delightful for words! All fled your benefactions as mice flee cats! And why? Not because people are ignorant and thankless as you imagined, but because in all your undertakings—forgive my frankness—there was not one spark of love or mercy. Only a wish to amuse yourself with living dolls! Nothing more! . . . A woman who doesn't know a man from a lapdog should not busy herself with charity. There is a great difference, I assure you, between men and lapdogs!"

The princess's heart beat quickly; the hammering rang in her ears; and again it seemed that the doctor would strike her with his hat. He spoke quickly, passionately, and without impressiveness; he stammered and gesticulated too much; and all she realised was that she listened to a rude, ill-tempered, ill-bred man; what he wanted to say and what he said, she failed to understand.

"Go away!" she said in a tearful voice, lifting her hands as if to ward off the doctor's hat. "Go away!"

"And how did you behave to your employés?" continued the doctor excitedly. "You treated them not as human beings, but worse than outcasts are treated. Allow me, for instance, to ask you why you got rid of me? I served faithfully ten years, first your father, then yourself, and I served honestly, without holiday or rest. I earned the love of all for a hundred versts around; and then . . . suddenly, one fine day, I am told I am wanted no more. And why? To this day I don't know. I, a doctor of medicine, a noble, a graduate of Moscow, the father of a family, I, it appears, am such an insignificant underling that I can be thrown out by the scruff of the neck without a word of explanation! Why make ceremony with me? I heard later that my wife, without my knowledge, went to you three times to petition for me, and that you did not receive her once. And she cried, I was told, in the

hall. And for that I will never forgive her, never! ...
never!"

The doctor stopped, and, grinding his teeth, tried
to find something more vindictive and painful. The
moment he succeeded, his cold, frowning face shone
with pleasure.

"Take your relations with this monastery!" he
began eagerly. " You spare no one, and the holier the
place the more certain it is to suffer from your charity
and angel ways. Why do you come here? What do
you want with these monks, let me ask? What is
Hecuba to you, and you to Hecuba? Again the same
broad farce, the same pose, the same scoffing at human
souls, and nothing more! You do not believe in these
monks' God; your heart has a god of its own discovered at spiritualist *séances;* on the Church's
mysteries you look condescendingly, you ignore the
services, you sleep till mid-day. . . . Why do you
come here? . . . Why to a strange monastery with
your own private god, imagining the monastery thinks
it a great honour? Ask yourself, if nothing else, what
your visits cost these monks! It pleased you to
come here to-day, so two days ago a horseman had to
be sent ahead to warn the monks. They spent all
yesterday preparing your rooms, and waiting. To-day
comes your advance-guard, an impudent serving-maid
who fusses about the yard, asks questions, orders
people about. . . . I cannot tolerate it. The monks

wasted all to-day looking out for you. If you're received without proper ceremony, woe to every one! You would complain to the Bishop. 'Your holiness, the monks don't love me! True, I am a great sinner; but I am so unhappy!' Already one monastery got a reprimand on your account. The Archimandrite here is a busy, studious man; he has not a moment free; yet you send for him to your rooms! No respect even for age and rank! ... If you did a lot for this monastery, there might be some excuse. But all this time the monks have not had a hundred roubles from you!"

When the princess was troubled, puzzled, or offended; when she was at a loss what to do, she usually wept. And here at last she covered her face, and cried a thin, childish cry. The doctor held his peace, and looked at her. His face darkened.

"Forgive me, princess," he said in a restrained voice. "I forgot myself, and gave way to wicked feelings. That was not right."

And with a confused cough, and his hat still in his hand, he walked quickly away.

The sky was already strewn with stars. The moon, it seemed, rose behind the monastery, for the sky above the roof was pale, transparent, and tender. Bats flew noiselessly past the white monastery walls.

The clock slowly struck three-quarters. It was a quarter to eight. The princess rose, and walked slowly

s

to the gate. She was offended, and cried; and it
seemed that trees and stars and bats felt pity for her,
and that the clock, chiming musically, showed its
compassion. She wept; and thought how good it
would be to enter the monastery for life; on still
summer evenings she would walk alone the garden
paths, offended, insulted, uncomprehended on earth,
with only God and the stars in heaven to see the
sufferer's tears. In the chapel the vesper service
continued. The princess stopped and listened to the
chanting; how fine these voices sounded in the
motionless, dark air! How sweet to weep and suffer,
and listen to these hymns!

When she returned to her rooms she looked at her
tear-stained face in a mirror, powdered it, and sat
down to supper. The monks knew how she loved
pickled sterlet, little mushrooms, Malaga, and simple
honey gingerbread which smelt of cypress in the
mouth; and each time she came they laid before her
these. As she ate the mushrooms and drank the Malaga, the princess thought that she would soon be
ruined and forsaken; that the stewards, agents, clerks,
and maids for whom she had done so much would
betray her, and speak to her insolently; that the whole
world would fall upon her, condemn her, turn her to
scorn; and that she would give up her title, luxury,
society, and retire to this monastery, uttering to no
one a word of reproach; that she would pray for her

enemies; that suddenly all would understand her, and
beg for forgiveness, but it would be too late. . . .

After supper she fell upon her knees in the ikon-
corner and read two chapters of the Gospel. Her
maid got ready her room, and she went to bed. The
princess stretched herself under the white counterpane,
sighed sweetly and deeply, as people sigh after tears,
then closed her eyes and went to sleep.

She awoke next morning, and looked at her watch:
it was half-past eight. Across the carpet fell a narrow,
bright belt of light, which came from the window but
barely lighted the room. Behind the black curtains
buzzed flies.

"It is early," she said to herself, and closed her
eyes.

She stretched herself, surrendered herself to the
feeling of comfort and cosiness; and recalled last
night's meeting with the doctor and the thoughts
which had lulled her to sleep; and she remembered
that she was unhappy. Her husband in St. Petersburg, her stewards, doctors, neighbours, official friends,
all returned to her. A long line of faces swept through
her imagination. She smiled softly, and thought that
if all these men could read her heart and understand
her, she would have them at her feet.

A quarter of an hour before midday she called her
maid.

"Come, dress me, Dasha!" she said lazily. "No . . .

first tell them to harness the horses. I am going to
Claudia Nikolaievna's."

Once outside her rooms the bright daylight made
her blink; and she smiled with pleasure—the day was
wonderfully fine. She looked through her blinking
eyes at the monks who crowded on the steps to see her
off; she nodded her head kindly and said—

"Good-bye, my friends! For two days only!"

It was a pleasant surprise also that the doctor came
to see her off. His face was pale and severe.

"Princess!" he began, with a guilty smile, taking
off his hat. "I have been waiting for you. . . .
Forgive me. . . . An evil, revengeful feeling carried
me away last night, and I talked . . . nonsense to
you. . . . I ask your pardon!"

The princess again smiled kindly, and offered her
hand. The doctor kissed it, and reddened.

Doing her best to look like a bird, the princess
swept into the carriage, and nodded her head to
all. In her heart again reigned joy, warmth, and
brightness; and she felt that her smile was more
than ever caressing and tender. As the carriage rolled
through the yard, then by the dusty road past huts
and gardens, past long carters' teams, past strings of
pilgrims on their way to prayer, she continued to
blink and smile. What greater joy, she reflected, than
to bring with oneself warmth and light and comfort, to
forgive offences, to smile kindly to foes. The road-

side peasants bowed, the *calèche* rocked easily; its wheels raised whirls of dust borne by the wind upon the golden rye; and the princess felt that she rocked not on the carriage cushions but on the clouds above, and that she herself was a light, transparent cloud.

"How happy I am!" she whispered, closing her eyes. "How happy I am!"

THE MUZHIKS

I

NIKOLAI TCHIKILDEYEFF, waiter, of the
Slaviansky Bazaar Hotel at Moscow, lost his
health. His numbed legs betrayed him, and once in
a corridor he stumbled and fell with a tray-load of
ham and peas. He had to throw up his work. What
money he had, his own and his wife's, soon went on
treatment; nothing remained to live on; he was
tired of idleness; and he saw that nothing remained
but to return to his native village. It was cheaper to
live at home, after all, and the best place for invalids;
and there is some truth in the proverb, "At home
even the walls help."

He arrived at Zhukovo towards evening. When
he recalled his childhood he pictured his birthplace as
bright, cosy, and comfortable; but now when he
entered the hut he felt something like fright, so dark,
so close, so dirty was it inside. And his wife Olga
and little daughter Sasha looked questioningly at the
big, untidy stove, black from smoke and flies, which
took up half the hut. What flies! The stove was

crooked, the logs in the walls sloped, and it seemed that every minute the hut would tumble to pieces. The ikon-corner, instead of pictures, was hung with bottle-labels and newspaper-cuttings. Poverty, poverty! Of the grown-ups no one was at home—they reaped in the fields; and alone on the stove sat an eight-year-old girl, fair-haired, unwashed, and so indifferent that she did not even look at the strangers. Beneath, a white cat rubbed herself against the pot-hanger.

"Puss, puss!" cried Sasha. "Pussy!"

"She can't hear," said the girl on the stove. "She's deaf!"

"How deaf?"

"Deaf. . . . From beating."

The first glance told Nikolai and Olga the life awaiting them; but they said nothing, silently laid down their bundles, and went into the street. The hut was the third from the corner, and the oldest and poorest in sight; its next-door neighbour, indeed, was little better; but the corner cabin boasted an iron roof and curtains in the windows. This cabin had no fence, and stood alone; it was the village inn. In one continuous row stretched other huts; and, as a whole, the village, peaceful and meditative, with the willows, elders, and mountain-ash peeping out of the gardens, was pleasing to see.

Behind the cabins the ground sloped steeply towards

the river; and here and there in the clay stuck denuded stones. On the slope, around these stones and the potters' pits, lay heaps of potsherds, some brown, some red; and below stretched a broad, flat, and bright green meadow, already mown, and now given over to the peasants' herds. A verst from the village ran the winding river with its pretty tufted banks; and beyond the river another field, a herd, long strings of white geese; then, as on the village side, a steep ascent. On the crest of the hill rose another village with a five-cupolaed church, and a little beyond it the local noble's house.

"It's a fine place, your village," said Olga, crossing herself towards the church. "What freedom, Lord!"

At that moment (it was Saturday night) the church bells rang for vesper service. In the valley beneath, two little girls with a water-pail turned their heads towards the church and listened to the bells.

"At the Slaviansky Bazaar they're sitting down to dinner," said Nikolai thoughtfully.

Seated on the brink of the ravine, Nikolai and Olga watched the setting sun and the image of the gold and purple sky in the river and in the church windows, and inhaled the soft, restful, inexpressibly pure air, unknown to them in Moscow. When the sun had set came lowing cattle and bleating sheep; geese flew towards them; and all was silent. The soft light faded from the air and evening shadows swept across the land.

Meantime the absent family returned to the hut. First came Nikolai's father and mother, dry, bent; and toothless, and of equal height. Later, their sons' wives, Marya and Fekla, employed on the noble's farm across the river. Marya, wife of Nikolai's brother Kiriak, had six children; Fekla, wife of Denis, then a soldier, two; and when Nikolai, entering the hut, saw the whole family, all these big and little bodies, which moved in the loft, in cradles, in corners; when he saw the greed with which the old man and women ate black bread soaked in water, he felt that he had made a mistake in coming home, sick, penniless, and—what was worse—with his family.

"And where is brother Kiriak?" he asked, greeting his parents.

"He's watchman at the trader's," answered the old man. "In the wood. He's a good lad, but drinks heavily."

"He's no profit," said the old woman in a lachrymose voice. "Our men are not much use, they bring nothing home with them, and only take things. Our Kiriak drinks; and the old man, there's no use hiding it, himself knows the way to the drink-shop. They've angered our Mother in Heaven!"

In honour of the guests the samovar was brought out. The tea smelt of fish, the sugar was damp and looked as if it had been gnawed, the bread and vessels were covered with cockroaches; it was painful to drink, and painful to hear the talk—of nothing but poverty and sickness. Before they had emptied their first glasses, from the yard came a loud, drawling, drunken cry—

"Ma-arya!"

"That sounds like Kiriak," said the old man. "Talk of the devil and he appears!"

The peasants were silent. A moment later came the same cry, rough and drawling, and this time it seemed to come from underground.

"Ma-arya!"

The elder daughter-in-law, Marya, turned deadly pale and pressed her body to the stove; and it was strange to see the expression of terror on the face of this strong, broad-shouldered, ugly woman. Her daughter, the little, indifferent girl who had sat on the stove, suddenly began to cry loudly.

"Stop howling, cholera!" cried angrily Fekla, a good-looking woman, also strong and broad-shouldered. "He won't kill you!"

From the old man Nikolai soon learned that Marya was afraid to live with her husband in the forest; and that when he had drunk too much Kiriak came for her, and made scenes and beat her mercilessly.

"Ma-arya!" came the cry, this time from outside the door.

"Help me, for the love of heaven, help me!" chattered Marya, breathing as if she had been thrown into icy water. "Help me, kinsmen——"

The houseful of children suddenly began to cry, and, seeing them, Sasha did the same. A drunken cough echoed without, and into the hut came a tall, black-bearded muzhik wearing a winter cap. In the dim lamp-light his face was barely visible, and all the more terrible. It was Kiriak. He went straight to his wife, flourished his arm, and struck her with his clenched fist in the face. Marya did not utter a sound, the blow seemed to have stunned her, but she seemed to dwindle; a stream of blood flowed out of her nose.

"It's a shame, a shame," muttered the old man, climbing on the stove. "And before our visitors! It's a sin!"

The old woman kept silence, and, bent in two, seemed lost in thought. Fekla rocked the cradle. Kiriak seized Marya's hand, dragged her to the door, and, to increase her terror, roared like a beast. But at that moment he saw the visitors, and stopped.

"So you've come!" he began, releasing his wife. "My own brother and his family. . . ."

He prayed a moment before the image, staggered, opened his red, drunken eyes, and continued—

"My brother and family have come to their parents' house . . . from Moscow, that means . . .

The old capital, that means, the city of Moscow, mother of cities. . . . Excuse . . ."

Amid the silence of all, he dropped on the bench near the samovar, and began to drink loudly from a saucer. When he had drunk ten cupfuls he leaned back on the bench and began to snore.

Bed-time came. Nikolai, as an invalid, was given a place on the stove beside the old man; Sasha slept on the floor; and Olga went with the young women to the shed.

"Never mind, my heart!" she said, lying on the hay beside Marya. "Crying is no help. You must bear it. In the Bible it is written, 'Whosoever shall smite thee on thy right cheek, turn to him the other also.' Don't cry, my heart!"

And then, in a whisper, she began to tell of Moscow, of her life there, how she had served as housemaid in furnished lodgings.

"In Moscow the houses a.e big and built of brick," said Olga. "There is no end of churches—forty forties of them—my heart; and the houses are all full of gentlemen, so good-looking, so smart!"

And Marya answered that she had never been in the district town, much less in Moscow; she was illiterate, and knew no prayers, not even "Our Father." Both she and her sister-in-law Fekla, who sat some way off and listened, were ignorant in the extreme, and understood nothing. Both disliked

their husbands; Marya dreaded Kiriak, shook with
terror when he stayed with her, and after his departure her head ached from the smell of vodka and
tobacco. And Fekla, in answer to the question did
she want her husband, answered angrily—

"What? . . . Him?"

For a time the women spoke, and then lay down.

It was cold, and a cock crew loudly, hindering
sleep. When the blue morning light began to break
through the chinks, Fekla rose stealthily and went
out, and her movements could be heard, as she ran
down the street in her bare feet.

II

When Olga went to church she took with her
Marya. As they descended the path to the meadow,
both were in good humour. Olga liked the freedom
of the country; and Marya found in her sister-in-
law a kindred spirit. The sun was rising. Close to
the meadow flew a sleepy hawk; the river was dull,
for there was a slight mist, but the hill beyond it
was bathed in light; the church glittered, and rooks
cawed in the garden of the big house beyond.

"The old man is not bad," said Marya. "But my
mother-in-law is cross and quarrelsome. Our own corn
lasted till Shrovetide; now we have to buy at the inn;

and the old woman is angry, and says, 'You eat too much.'"

"Never mind, my heart! You must bear that too. It is written in the Bible, 'Come unto Me all ye that are weary and heavy laden.'"

Olga spoke gravely and slowly; and walked, like a pilgrim, quickly and briskly. Every day she read the Gospel, aloud, like a clerk; and though there was much that she did not understand, the sacred words touched her to tears, and words like *astche, dondezhe* she pronounced with beating heart. She believed in God, in the Virgin, in the saints; and her faith was that it was wrong to do evil to any man, even to Germans, gipsies, and Jews. When she read aloud the Gospel, even when she stopped at words she did not understand, her face grew compassionate, kindly, and bright.

"What part are you from?" asked Marya.

"Vladimir. I have been long in Moscow, since I was eight years old."

They approached the river. On the other bank stood a woman, undressing herself.

"That is our Fekla!" said Marya. "She's been across the river at the squire's house. With the stewards! She's impudent and ill-spoken—awful!"

Black-browed Fekla, with loosened hair, jumped into the river, and, young and firm as a girl, splashed in the water, making big waves.

T

"She's impudent—awful!" repeated Marya.

Across the river was a shaky bridge of beams, and at that moment beneath it in the clear, transparent water swam carp. On the green bushes, imaged in the water, glistened dew. It was warm and pleasant. What a wonderful morning! And indeed, how splendid would be life in this world were it not for poverty, hideous, hopeless poverty, from which there is no escape! But look back to the village, and memory awakens all the events of yesterday; and the intoxication of joy vanishes in a wink.

The women reached the church. Marya stopped near the door, afraid to go inside. She feared, too, to sit down, though the service would not begin till nine o'clock, and stood all the time.

As the Gospel was being read the worshippers suddenly moved, and made way for the squire's family. In came two girls in white dresses with wide-brimmed hats, and behind them a stout, rosy boy dressed as a sailor. Their coming pleased Olga; she felt that here at last were well-taught, orderly, good-looking people. But Marya looked at them furtively and gloomily, as if they were not human beings but monsters who would crush her if she failed to make way.

And when the deacon sang out in a bass voice, she fancied she heard the cry "Ma-arya!" and shuddered.

III

The village quickly heard of the visitors' arrival, and when church was over the hut was crowded. The Leonuitcheffs, Matveitcheffs, and Ilitchoffs came for news of their kinsmen in Moscow. Every man in Zhukovo who could read and write was taken to Moscow as waiter or boots; and, similarly, the village across the river supplied only bakers; and this custom obtained since before the Emancipation, when a certain legendary Luka Ivanuitch, of Zhukovo, was lord of the buffet in a Moscow club, and hired none but fellow-villagers. These, in turn attaining power, sent for their kinsmen and found them posts in inns and restaurants; so that from that time Zhukovo was called by the local population Khamskaya[1] or Kholuefka.[1] Nikolai was taken to Moscow at the age of eleven, and given a post by Ivan Makaruitch, one of the Matveitcheffs, then porter at the Hermitage Gardens. And, now, turning to the Matveitcheffs, Nikolai said gravely—

"Ivan Makaruitch was my benefactor; it is my duty to pray God for him day and night, for it was through him I became a good man."

"*Batiushka* mine!" said tearfully a tall, old woman,

[1] Derived from *Kham* and *Kholui*, words expressing subjection and abasement.

Ivan Makaruitch's sister. "And have you no news of him?"

"He was at Omon's last winter; and this season, I heard, he's in some gardens outside town. . . . He's grown old. Once in the summer he'd bring home ten roubles a day, but now everywhere business is dull—the old man's in a bad way."

The women, old and young, looked at the high felt boots on Nikolai's legs, and at his pale face, and said sadly—

"You're no money-maker, Nikolai Osipuitch, no money-bringer!"

And all caressed Sasha. Sasha was past her tenth birthday, but, small and very thin, she looked not more than seven. Among the sunburnt, untidy village girls, in their long cotton shirts, pale-faced, big-eyed Sasha, with the red ribbon in her hair, seemed a toy, a little strange animal caught in the fields, and brought back to the hut.

"And she knows how to read!" boasted Olga, looking tenderly at her daughter. "Read something, child!" she said, taking a New Testament from the corner. "Read something aloud and let the ortho-dox listen!"

The old, heavy, leather-bound, bent-edged Bible smelt like a monk. Sasha raised her eyebrows, and began in a loud drawl—

". . . And when they were departed, behold the

angel of the Lord appeareth to Joseph in a dream, saying, Arise and take the young child and his mother . . ."

"'The young child and his mother,'" repeated Olga. She reddened with joy.
until I bring thee word. . . ."

". . . and flee into Egypt . . . and be thou there

At the word "until" Olga could not longer restrain her emotion and began to cry. Marya followed her example, and Ivan Makaruitch's sister cried also. The old man coughed and fussed about, seeking a present for his grandchild, but he found nothing, and waved his hand. When the reading ended, the visitors dispersed to their homes, deeply touched, and pleased with Olga and Sasha.

As the day was Sunday the family remained in the hut. The old woman, whom husband, daughters-in-law, and grandchildren alike addressed as "grandmother," did everything with her own hands: she lighted the stove, set the samovar; she even worked in the fields; and at the same time growled that she was tortured with work. She tortured herself with dread that the family might eat too much, and took care that her husband and daughters-in-law did not sit with idle hands. Once when she found that the innkeeper's geese had got into her kitchen-garden, she rushed at once out of the house armed with a long stick; and for half an hour screamed

piercingly over her cabbages, which were as weak
and thin as their owner. Later she imagined that
a hawk had swooped on her chickens, and with loud
curses she flew to meet the hawk. She lost her
temper and growled from morning to night, and
often screamed so loudly that passers-by stopped to
listen.

Her husband she treated badly, denouncing him
sometimes as a lie-abed, sometimes as "cholera."
The old man was a hopeless, unsubstantial muzhik,
and perhaps, indeed, if she had not spurred him
on, he would have done no work at all, but sat all
day on the stove and talked. He complained to his
son at great length of certain enemies in the village
and of the wrongs he suffered day by day; and it
was tiresome to hear him.

"Yes," he said, putting his arms to his waist.
"Yes. A week after Elevation I sold my hay for
thirty kopecks a pood. Yes. Good! . . . and this means
that one morning I drive my hay cart and inter-
fere with nobody; and suddenly, in an evil moment,
I look round, and out of the inn comes the headman,
Antip Siedelnikoff. 'Where are you driving, old So-
and-so?' and bangs me in the ear!"

Kiriak's head ached badly from drink, and he was
ashamed before his brother.

"It's drink that does it. *Akh*, my Lord God!"
he stammered, shaking his big head. "You, brother

and you, sister, forgive me, for the love of Christ; I feel bad myself."

To celebrate Sunday, they bought herrings at the inn, and made soup of the heads. At midday all sat down to tea and drank until they sweated and, it seemed, swelled up; and when they had drunk the tea they set to on the soup, all eating from the same bowl. The old woman hid away the herrings.

At night a potter baked his pots in the ravine. In the meadow below, the village girls sang in chorus; and some one played a concertina. Beyond the river also glowed a potter's oven, and village girls sang; and from afar the music sounded soft and harmonious. The muzhiks gathered in the inn; they sang tipsily, each a different song; and the language they used made Olga shudder and exclaim—

"*Akh, batiushki!*"

She was astonished by the incessant blasphemy, and by the fact that the older men, whose time had nearly come, blasphemed worst of all. And the children and girls listened to this language, and seemed in no way uncomfortable; it was plain they were used to it, and had heard it from the cradle.

Midnight came; the potters' fires on both river-banks went out, but on the meadow below and in the inn the merry-making continued. The old man and Kiriak, both drunk, holding hands, and rolling against one another, came to the shed where Olga lay with Marya.

"Leave her alone!" reasoned the old man. "Leave her. She's not a bad sort. . . . It's a sin. . . ."

"Ma-arya!" roared Kiriak.

"Stop! It's sinful. . . . She's not a bad sort."

The two men stood a moment by the shed and went away.

"I love wild flowers . . ." sang the old man in a high, piercing tenor. "I love to pull them in the fields!"

After this he spat, blasphemed, and went into the hut.

IV

Grandmother stationed Sasha in the kitchen garden, and ordered her to keep off the geese. It was a hot August day. The innkeeper's geese could get into the kitchen garden by the back way, but at present they were busy picking up oats near the inn and quietly conversing, though the old gander stood aloof, his head raised as if to make sure that grandmother was not coming with her stick. The other geese could also get into the garden; but these were feeding far across the river, and, like a big white garland, stretched across the meadow. Sasha watched a short time, and then got tired, and, seeing no geese in sight, went down to the ravine.

There she saw Motka, Marya's eldest daughter, standing motionless on a big stone, and looking at the church. Marya had borne thirteen children; but only six remained, all girls, and the eldest was eight years old. Bare-footed Motka, in her long shirt, stood in the sun; the sun burnt the top of her head, but she took no notice of this, and seemed turned to stone. Sasha stood beside her, and looking at the church, began—

"God lives in the church. People burn lamps and candles, but God has red lamps, green and blue lamps, like eyes. At night God walks about the church, and with him the Holy Virgin, and holy Nicholas . . . toup, toup, toup! . . . The watchman is frightened, terribly! Yes, my heart," she said, imitating her mother. "When the Day of Judgment comes all the churches will be carried up to heaven."

"With the bells?" asked Motka in a bass voice, drawling every word.

"With the bells. And on the Day of Judgment good people will go to paradise, and wicked people will burn in fire eternal and unextinguishable, my heart! To mother and Marya God will say, 'You have offended no one, so go to the right, to paradise'; but He'll say to Kiriak and grandmother, 'You go to the left, into the fire!' And people who eat meat on fast-days will go to the fire too."

She looked up at the sky, opened wide her eyes, and continued—

"Look up at the sky, don't wink . . . and you'll see angels."

Motka looked at the sky, and a minute passed in silence.

"Do you see them?" asked Sasha.

"No," answered Motka in her bass voice.

"But I can. Little angels fly about the sky, with wings . . . little, little, like gnats."

Motka thought a moment, looked at the ground, and asked—

"Will grandmother burn really?"

"She'll burn, my heart."

From the stone to the bottom of the hill was a gentle, even slope covered with green grass so soft that it invited repose. Sasha lay down and slid to the bottom. Motka with a serious, severe face, puffed out her cheeks, lay down, and slid, and as she slid her shirt came up to her shoulders.

"How funny I felt!" said Sasha in delight.

The two children climbed to the top intending to slide down again, but at that moment they heard a familiar, squeaky voice. Terror seized them. Toothless, bony, stooping grandmother, with her short grey hair floating in the wind, armed with the long stick, drove the geese from the kitchen garden, and screamed—

"You've spoiled all the cabbage, accursed; may you choke; threefold anathemas; plagues, there is no peace with you!"

She saw the two girls, threw down her stick, took up a bundle of brushwood, and seizing Sasha's shoulders with fingers dry and hard as tree-forks, began to beat her. Sasha cried from pain and terror; and at that moment a gander, swinging from foot to foot and stretching out its neck, came up and hissed at the old woman; and when he returned to the geese, all welcomed him approvingly: go-go-go! Thereafter grandmother seized and whipped Motka, and again Motka's shirt went over her shoulders. Trembling with terror, crying loudly, Sasha went back to the hut to complain, and after her went Motka, also crying in her bass voice. Her tears were unwiped away, and her face was wet as if she had been in the river.

"Lord in heaven!" cried Olga as they entered the hut. "Mother of God, what's this?"

Sasha began her story, and at that moment, screaming and swearing, in came grandmother. Fekla lost her temper, and the whole hut was given over to noise.

"Never mind, never mind!" consoled Olga, pale and unnerved, stroking Sasha's head. "She's your grandmother; you've no right to be angry. Never mind, child!"

Nikolai, already tortured by the constant shouting, hunger, smell, and smoke, hating and despising poverty, and ashamed of his parents before his wife and child, swung his legs over the stove and said to his mother with an irritable whine—

"You mustn't touch her! You have no right whatever to beat her!"

"Nu, you'll choke there on the stove, corpse!" cried Fekla angrily. "The devil sent you to us, parasite!"

And Sasha and Motka, and all the little girls, hid on the stove behind Nikolai's back, and the throbbing of their little hearts was almost heard. In every family with an invalid, long sick and hopeless, there are moments when all, timidly, secretly, at the bottom of their hearts, wish for his death; alone, children always dread the death of any one kin to them, and feel terror at the thought. And now the little girls, with bated breath and mournful faces, looked at Nikolai, and thinking that he would soon die, wanted to cry and say something kindly and compassionate.

Nikolai pressed close to Olga, as if seeking a defender, and said in a soft, trembling voice—

"Olga, my dear, I can stand this no longer. It is beyond my strength. For the love of God, for the love of Christ in heaven, write to your sister, Claudia Abramovna; let her sell or pledge every-

thing, and send us the money to get out of this.
O Lord," he cried, with longing, "to look at Moscow
again, even with one eye! Even to see it in dreams!"

When evening came and the hut grew dark, all
felt such tedium that it was hard to speak. Angry
grandmother soaked rye crusts in a bowl, and took
an hour to eat them. Marya milked the cow, carried
in the milk-pail, and set it down on a bench; and
grandmother slowly poured the milk into jugs, pleased
at the thought that now at Assumption fast no one
would drink milk, and that it would remain whole.
But she poured a little, very little, into a saucer for
Fekla's youngest. When she and Marya carried the
milk to the cellar Motka suddenly started up, climbed
down from the stove, and going to the bench poured
the saucer of milk into the wooden bowl of crusts.

Grandmother, back in the hut, sat down again to
the crusts, and Sasha and Motka, perched on the
stove, looked at her, and saw with joy that she was
drinking milk during fast time, and therefore would
go to hell. Consoled by this, they lay down to sleep;
and Sasha, going off to sleep, imagined the terrible
chastisement: a big stove, like the potter's, and a
black unclean spirit horned like a cow drove grandmother into the stove with a long stick, as she herself
had lately driven the geese.

V

On the night of Assumption, at eleven o'clock, the young men and girls playing below in the meadow suddenly cried and shrieked and ran back towards the village. The boys and girls who sat above, on the brink of the ravine, at first could not understand the cause of their cries.

"Fire! Fire!" came from beneath in a despairing scream! "The hut's on fire!"

The boys and girls on the ravine turned their heads and saw a picture terrible and rare. Over one of the farthest thatched huts rose a fathom-high pillar of fire which curled and scattered fountain-wise on all sides showers of bright sparks. And immediately afterwards the whole roof caught fire, and the crackling of burning beams was heard by all.

The moonlight faded, and soon the whole village was bathed in a red, trembling glare; black shadows moved across the ground, and there was a smell of burning. The merry-makers from below, all panting, speechless, shuddering, jostled one another and fell; dazzled by the bright light, they saw nothing, and could not even tell who was who. The sight was terrible; and most terrible of all was that in the smoke above the conflagration fluttered doves, and that the men in the inn, knowing nothing of the fire, continued to sing and play the concertina as if nothing had happened.

"Uncle Semion is burning!" cried a loud, hoarse voice.

Marya with chattering teeth wandered about her hut weeping and wringing her hands, although the fire was far away at the other end of the village; Nikolai came out in his felt boots, and after him the children in their shirts. At the village policeman's hut they beat the alarm. Bem, bem, bem! echoed through the air; and this tireless, repeated sound made the heart sink and the listeners turn cold. The old women stood about with images. From the yards were driven sheep, calves, and cows; and the villagers carried into the street their boxes, sheepskins, and pails. A black stallion, kept apart from the herd because he kicked and injured the horses, found himself in freedom, and neighing loudly, he tore up and down the village, and at last stopped beside a cart and kicked it violently.

In the church beyond the river the fire-alarm was rung.

It was hot all around the burning hut, and in the bright glare even the blades of grass were visible. On a box which the peasants had managed to save sat Semion, a big-nosed, red-headed muzhik, in short coat, with a forage-cap pressed down to his ears; his wife lay on her face on the earth and groaned. A little, big-bearded, capless, gnome-like stranger of eighty, evidently partial to fires, wandered around, carrying a white bundle; his bald head reflected the glare. The *starosta*, Antip Siedelnikoff, swarthy and black-haired as a gipsy, went up to the hut with his axe, and for no apparent reason beat in all the windows and began to hack at the steps.

"Women, water!" he roared. "Bring the engine! Look sharp!"

The peasants, fresh from merry-making in the inn, dragged up the fire-engine. All were drunk; they staggered and fell; their expressions were helpless, and tears stood in their eyes.

"Bring water, girls!" cried the *starosta*, also drunk. "Look sharp!"

The young women and girls ran down the slope to the well, returned with pails and pitchers of water, and, having emptied them into the engine, ran back for more. Olga, and Marya, and Sasha, and Motka, all helped. The water was pumped up by women and small boys; the hose-nozzle hissed; and the *starosta*, aiming it now at the door, now at the windows, held his finger on the stream of water, so that it hissed still more fiercely.

"Good man, Antip!" came approving cries. "Keep it up!"

And Antip went into the hall and cried thence—

"Bring more water! Do your best, Orthodox men and women, on this unfortunate occasion!"

The muzhiks stood in a crowd with idle hands and gaped at the fire. Not one knew what to start on, not one was capable of help; although around were stacks of grain, hay, outhouses, and heaps of dry brushwood. Kiriak and his father Osip, both tipsy, stood in the crowd. As if to excuse his idleness, the old man turned to the woman who lay on the ground and said—

"Don't worry yourself, gossip! The hut's insured—it's all the same to you!"

And Semion, addressing each muzhik in turn, explained how the hut caught fire.

"That old man there with the bundle is General Zhukoff's servant. . . . He was with our general, heaven kingdom to him! as cook. He comes up to us in the evening and begins, 'Let me sleep here to-night.' . . . We had a drink each, of course. . . . The woman prepared the samovar to get the old man tea, when in an unlucky moment she put it in the hall; and the fire from the chimney, of course, went up to the roof, the straw and all! We were nearly burnt ourselves. And the old man lost his cap; it's a pity."

The fire-alarm boomed without cease; and the bells of the church across the river rang again and again. Olga, panting, bathed in the glare, looked with terror

U

at the red sheep and the red pigeons flying about in
the smoke; and it seemed to her that the boom of the
fire-alarm pierced into her soul, that the fire would
last for ever, and that Sasha was lost. . . . And when
the roof crashed in she grew so weak with fear lest
the whole village burn that she could no longer carry
water; and she sat on the brink of the ravine with her
pail beside her; beside her sat other women, and spoke
as if they were speaking of a corpse.

At last from the manor-house came two cartloads of
factors and workmen. They brought with them a fire-
engine. A very youthful student in white, unbuttoned
tunic rode into the village on horseback. Axes
crashed, a ladder was placed against the burning log-
walls; and up it promptly climbed five men led by the
student, who was very red, and shouted sharply and
hoarsely, and in a tone which implied that he was well
accustomed to extinguishing fires. They took the hut
to pieces, beam by beam; and dragged apart stall, the
wattle fence, and the nearest hayrick.

" Don't let them break it ! " came angry voices from
the crowd. " Don't let them ! "

Kiriak with a resolute face went into the hut as if to
prevent the new-comers breaking, but one of the workmen turned him back with a blow on the neck. Kiriak
tumbled, and on all fours crept back to the crowd.

From across the river came two pretty girls in hats;
the student's sisters, no doubt. They stood some way

off and watched the conflagration. The scattered logs no longer burned, but smoked fiercely; and the student, handling the hose, sent the water sometimes on the logs, sometimes into the crowd, sometimes at the women who were carrying pails.

"George!" cried the frightened girls reproachfully. "George!"

The fire ended. Before the crowd dispersed the dawn had begun; and all faces were pale and a little dark—or so it always seems in early morning when the last stars fade away. As they went to their homes the muzhiks laughed and joked at the expense of General Zhukoff's cook and his burnt cap: they re-enacted the fire as a joke, and, it seemed, were sorry it had come so quickly to an end.

"You put out the fire beautifully, sir," said Olga to the student. "Quite in the Moscow way; there we have fires every day."

"Are you really from Moscow?" asked one of the girls.

"Yes. My husband served in the Slaviansky Bazaar. And this is my little girl." She pointed to Sasha, who pressed close to her from the cold. "Also from Moscow, miss."

The girls spoke to the student in French, and handed Sasha a twenty-kopeck piece. When old Osip saw this his face grew bright with hope.

"Thank God, your honour, there was no wind," he

said, turning to the student. "We'd have been all
burnt up in an hour. Your honour, good gentleman,"
he added shamefacedly. "It's a cold morning; we want
warming badly . . . a half a bottle from your kindness . . ."

Osip's hint proved vain; and, grunting, he staggered
home. Olga stood at the end of the village and
watched as the two carts forded the stream, and the
pretty girls walked through the meadow towards the
carriage waiting on the other side. She returned to
the hut in ecstasies—

"And such nice people! So good-looking. The
young ladies, just like little cherubs!"

"May they burst asunder!" growled sleepy Fekla
angrily.

VI

Marya was unhappy, and said that she wanted to
die. But life as she found it was quite to Fekla's
taste: she liked the poverty, and the dirt, and the never-
ceasing bad language. She ate what she was given without picking and choosing, and could sleep comfortably
anywhere; she emptied the slops in front of the steps:
threw them, in fact, from the threshold, though in her
own naked feet she had to walk through the puddle.
And from the first day she hated Olga and Nikolai for
no reason save that they loathed this life.

"We'll see what you're going to eat here, my nobles from Moscow!" she said maliciously. "We'll see!"

Once on an early September morning, Fekla, rosy from the cold, healthy, and good-looking, carried up the hill two pails of water; when she entered the hut Marya and Olga sat at the table and drank tea.

"Tea . . . and sugar!" began Fekla ironically. "Fine ladies you are!" she added, setting down the pails. "A nice fashion you've got of drinking tea every day! See that you don't swell up with tea!" she continued, looking with hatred at Olga. "You got a thick snout already in Moscow, fatbeef!"

She swung round the yoke and struck Olga on the shoulder. The two women clapped their hands and exclaimed—

"*Akh, batiushki!*"

After which Fekla returned to the river to wash clothes, and all the time cursed so loudly that she was heard in the hut.

The day passed, and behind it came the long autumn evening. All sat winding silk, except Fekla, who went down to the river. The silk was given out by a neighbouring factory; and at this work the whole family earned not more than twenty kopecks a week.

"We were better off as serfs," said the old man, winding away busily. "In those days you'd work, and eat, and sleep . . . each in its turn. For dinner you'd have *schtchi*[1] and porridge, and for supper again *schtchi* and porridge. Gherkins and cabbage as much as you liked; and you'd eat freely, as much as you liked. And there was more order. Each man knew his place."

The one lamp in the hut burned dimly and smoked. When any worker rose and passed the lamp a black shadow fell on the window, and the bright moonlight shone in. Old Osip related slowly how the peasants lived before the Emancipation; how in these same villages where all to-day lived penuriously there were great shooting parties, and on such days the muzhiks were treated to vodka without end; how whole trains of carts with game for the young squire were hurried off to Moscow; how the wicked were punished with rods or exiled to the estate in Tver, and the good were rewarded. And grandmother also spoke. She remembered everything. She told of her old mistress, a good, God-fearing woman with a wicked, dissolute husband; and of the queer marriages made by all the daughters: one, it appeared, married a drunkard; another a petty tradesman; and the third was carried off clandestinely (she, grandmother, then unmarried, helped in the adventure): and all soon afterwards died of grief, as died, indeed, their mother. And, remembering these events, grandmother began to cry.

When a knock was heard at the door all started.

[1] Cabbage soup.

"Uncle Osip, let me stay the night!"

Into the hut came the little, bald old man, General Zhukoff's cook, whose cap was burnt in the fire. He sat and listened, and, like his hosts, related many strange happenings. Nikolai, his legs hanging over the stove, listened; and asked what sort of food was eaten at the manor-house. They spoke of *bitki*, cutlets, soups of various kinds, and sauces; and the cook, who, too, had an excellent memory, named certain dishes which no one eats nowadays; there was a dish, for instance, made of ox-eyes, and called "Awake in the morning."

"And did you cook cutlets *maréchal?*" asked Nikolai.

"No."

Nikolai shook his head reproachfully, and said—

"Then you are a queer sort of cook."

The little girls sat and lay on the stove, and looked down with widely opened eyes; there seemed to be no end to them—like cherubs in the sky. The stories delighted them; they sighed, shuddered, and turned pale, sometimes from rapture, sometimes from fear; and, breathless, afraid to move, they listened to the stories of their grandmother, which were the most interesting of all.

They went to bed in silence; and the old men, agitated by their stories, thought how glorious was youth, which—however meagre it might be—left behind it only joyful, living, touching recollections; and how terribly cold was this death, which was now so near. Better not think of it! The lamp went out. And the darkness, the two windows, bright with moonshine, the silence, the cradle's creak somehow reminded them that life was now past, and that it would never return. They slumbered, lost consciousness; then suddenly some one jostled their shoulders, or breathed into their cheeks—and there was no real sleep; through their heads crept thoughts of death; they turned round and forgot about death; but their heads were full of old, mean, tedious thoughts, thoughts of need, of forage, of the rise in the price of flour; and again they remembered that life had now passed by, and that it would never return.

"O Lord!" sighed the cook.

Some one tapped cautiously at the window. That must be Fekla. Olga rose, yawned, muttered a prayer, opened the inner door, then drew the bolt in the hall. But no one entered. A draught blew and the moon shone brightly. Through the open door, Olga saw the quiet and deserted street, and the moon itself, swimming high in the sky.

"Who's there?" she cried.

"I!" came a voice. "It's I."

Near the door, pressing close to the wall, stood Fekla, naked as she was born. She shuddered from

the cold, her teeth chattered; and in the bright
moonlight she was pale, pretty, and strange. The
patches of shade and the moonlight on her skin
stood out sharply; and plainest of all stood out her
dark eyebrows and her young, firm breast.

"Some impudent fellows across the river undressed
me and sent me off in this way—as my mother bore
me! Bring me something to put on."

"Go into the hut yourself!" whispered Olga, with
a shudder.

"The old ones will see me.".

And as a fact grandmother got restless, and
growled; and the old man asked, "Who is there?"
Olga brought out her shift and petticoat and dressed
Fekla; and the two women softly, and doing their
best to close the doors without noise, went into the
hut.

"So that's you, devil?" came an angry growl from
grandmother, who guessed that it was Fekla. "May
you be . . . night walker . . . there's no peace with
you!"

"Don't mind, don't mind," whispered Olga, wrapping Fekla up. "Don't mind, my heart!"

Again silence. The whole family always slept
badly; each was troubled by something aggressive
and insistent: the old man by a pain in the back;
grandmother by worry and ill-temper; Marya by
fright; the children by itching and hunger. And

to-night the sleep of all was troubled; they rolled from side to side, wandered, and rose constantly to drink.

Fekla suddenly cried out in a loud, rough voice; but soon mastered herself, and merely sobbed quietly until at last she ceased. Now and then from beyond the river were heard the church chimes; but the clock struck strangely; and at first beat struck five, and later three.

"O Lord!" sighed the cook.

From the light in the windows it was hard to judge whether the moon still shone or whether dawn had come. Marya rose and went out; and she was heard milking the cows and shouting "Stand!" Grandmother also went out. It was still dark in the hut, but everything could be seen.

Nikolai, who had spent a sleepless night, climbed down from the stove. He took from a green box his evening dress-coat, put it on, and going over to the window, smoothed the sleeves and the folds, and smiled. Then he took off the coat, returned it to the box, and lay down.

Marya returned, and began to light the stove. Apparently she was not yet quite awake. Probably she still dreamed of something, or recalled the stories of last night, for she stretched herself lazily before the stove and said—

"No, we're better in freedom."

VII

In the village arrived "the gentleman," as the peasants called the superintendent of police. Every one knew a week ahead the day and cause of his arrival. For though Zhukovo had only forty houses, it owed in arrears to the Imperial Treasury and the Zemstvo more than two thousand roubles.

The superintendent stopped at the inn, drank two glasses of tea, and then walked .to the *starosta's* hut, where already waited a crowd of peasants in arrear. The *starosta*, Antip Siedelnikoff, despite his youth—he was little over thirty—was a stern man who always took the side of the authorities, although he himself was poor and paid his taxes irregularly. It was clear to all that he was flattered by his position and revelled in the sense of power, which he had no other way of displaying save by sternness. The *mir* feared and listened to him; when in the street. or at the .inn he met a drunken .man he would .seize him, tie his hands behind his back, and put him in the village gaol; once, indeed, he even imprisoned grandmother for several days, because, appearing at the *mir* instead of her husband, she used abusive language. The *starosta* had never lived in town and read no books; but he had a copious collection of learned words and used them so liberally that people respected him, even when they did not understand.

When Osip with his tax book entered the *starosta's* hut, the superintendent, a thin, old, grey-whiskered man in a grey coat, sat at a table in the near corner and made notes in a book. The hut was clean, the walls were decorated with pictures from magazines, and in a prominent place near the ikon hung a portrait of Alexander of Battenberg, ex-Prince of Bulgaria. At the table, with crossed arms, stood Antip Siedelnikoff.

"This man, your honour, owes 119 roubles," he said when it came to Osip's turn. "Before Holy Week he paid a rouble, since then, nothing."

The superintendent turned his eyes on Osip, and asked—

"What's the reason of that, brother?"

"Your honour, be merciful to me . . ." began Osip in agitation. "Let me explain . . . this summer . . . Squire Liutoretzky . . . 'Osip,' he says, 'sell me your hay. . . . Sell it,' he says. . . . I had a hundred poods for sale, which the women mowed. . . . Well, we bargained. . . . All went well, without friction. . . ."

He complained of the *starosta*, and now and again turned to the muzhiks as if asking for support; his flushed face sweated, and his eyes turned bright and vicious.

"I don't understand why you tell me all that," said the superintendent. "I ask *you* . . . it's *you* I ask, why you don't pay your arrears? None of you pay, and I am held responsible."

"I'm not able to."

"These expressions are without consequence, your honour," said the *starosta* magniloquently. "In reality, the Tchikildeyeffs belong to the impoverished class, but be so good as to ask the others what is the reason. Vodka and impudence . . . without any comprehension."

The superintendent made a note, and said to Osip in a quiet, even voice, as if he were asking for water—

"Begone!"

Soon afterwards he drove away; and as he sat in his cheap tarantass and coughed, it was plain, even from the appearance of his long, thin back, that he had forgotten Osip, and the *starosta*, and the arrears of Zhukovo, and was thinking of his own domestic affairs. He had hardly covered a verst before Antip Siedelni-koff was carrying off the Tchikildeyeff's samovar; and after him ran grandmother, and whined like a dog.

"I won't give it! I won't give it to you, accursed!"

The *starosta* walked quickly, taking big steps; and grandmother, stooping and fierce and breathless, tottered after him; and her green-grey hair floated in the wind. At last she stopped, beat her breast with her fists, and exclaimed, with a whine and a sob—

"Orthodox men who believe in God! *Batiushki*, they're wronging me! Kinsmen, they've robbed me. Oi, oi, will no one help me!"

"Grandmother, grandmother!" said the *starosta* severely, "have some reason in your head!"

With the loss of the samovar, things in the Tchikildeyeffs' hut grew even worse. There was something humiliating and shameful in this last privation, and it seemed that the hut had suddenly lost its honour. The table itself, the chairs, and all the pots, had the *starosta* seized them, would have been less missed. Grandmother screamed, Marya cried, and the children, listening, began to cry also. The old man, with a feeling of guilt, sat gloomily in the corner and held his tongue. And Nikolai was silent. As a rule grandmother liked him and pitied him; but at this crisis her pity evaporated, and she cursed and reproached him, and thrust her fists under his nose. She screamed that he was guilty of the family's misfortunes and asked why he had sent so little home, though he boasted in his letters that he earned fifty roubles a month at the Slaviansky Bazaar. Why did he come home, and, still worse, bring his family? If he died whence would the money come for his funeral? . . . And it was painful to look at Nikolai, Olga, and Sasha.

The old man grunted, took his cap, and went to the *starosta's*. It was getting dark. Antip Siedelnikoff,

with cheeks puffed out, stood at the stove and soldered.
It was stifling. His children, skinny and unwashed—
no better than the Tchikildeyeffs'—sprawled on the
floor; his ugly, freckled wife wound silk. This, too,
was an unhappy, God-forsaken family; alone Antip
was smart and good-looking. On a bench in a row
stood five samovars. The old man prayed towards the
Battenberg prince, and began—

"Antip, show the mercy of God: give me the
samovar! For the love of God!"

"Bring me three roubles, and then you'll get it."

"I haven't got them."

Antip puffed out his cheeks, the fire hummed and
hissed, and the samovars shone. The old man fumbled
with his cap, thought a moment, and repeated—

"Give it to me!"

The swarthy *starosta* seemed quite black and resembled a wizard; he turned to Osip and said roughly
and quickly—

"All depends from the Rural Chief. In the ad-
ministrative session of the twenty-sixth of this month
you can expose the causes of your dissatisfaction
verbally or in writing."

Not one of these learned words was understood by
Osip, but he felt contented, and returned to his hut.

Ten days later the superintendent returned, stayed
about an hour, and drove away. It had turned windy
and cold, but though the river was frozen, there was

no snow, and the state of the roads was a torture to every one. On Sunday evening the neighbours looked in to see and talk with Osip. They spoke in the darkness; to work was a sin, and no one lighted the lamp. News was exchanged, chiefly disagreeable. Three houses away the hens had been taken in payment of arrears and sent to the cantonal office, and there they died of starvation; sheep had also been taken, and while they were being driven away tied with ropes and transferred to fresh carts at each village one had died. And now they discussed the question, Who was responsible?

"The Zemstvo!" said Osip. "Who else?"

"Of course, the Zemstvo!"

They accused the Zemstvo of everything—of arrears, of oppression, of famines, although not one of them knew exactly what the Zemstvo was. And that rule had been observed since wealthy peasants with factories, shops, and houses were elected as Zemstvo members, and being discontented with the institution, thenceforth in their factories and inns abused the Zemstvo.

They complained of the fact that God had sent no snow, and that though it was time to lay in firewood, you could neither drive nor walk upon the frozen roads. Fifteen years before, and earlier, the small-talk of Zhukovo was infinitely more entertaining. In those days every old man pretended he held some secret, knew something, and waited for something; they talked of rescripts with gold seals, redistribution of lands, and hidden treasures, and hinted of things mysterious; to-day the people of Zhukovo had no secrets; their life was open to all; and they had no themes for conversation save need, and forage, and the absence of snow. . . .

For a moment they were silent. But soon they remembered the hens and dead sheep, and returned to the problem, Who was responsible?

"The Zemstvo!" said Osip gloomily. "Who else?"

VIII

The parish church was Kosogorovo, six versts away, but the peasants went there only to christen, marry, or bury; they worshipped at the church across the river. On Sundays, when the weather was fine, the village girls dressed in their best and went in a crowd to the service; and the red, yellow, and green dresses fluttering across the meadow were pleasant to see. In bad weather all stayed at home. They fasted, prayed, and prepared for the sacrament. From those who had failed in this duty during the Great Fast, the priest, when he went round the huts with his crucifix, took fifteen kopecks fine.

The old man did not believe in God, because he

x

had hardly ever thought of Him; he admitted the supernatural, but held that that was an affair for women; and when others spoke of religion, or of miracles, and asked him questions on the subject, he scratched himself and said reluctantly—

" Who knows anything about it ?"

Grandmother believed vaguely; in her mind all things were confused, and when she began to meditate on death and salvation, hunger and poverty took the upper hand, and she forgot her meditations. She remembered no prayers, but at night before lying down she stood before the ikons and muttered—

"Mother of God of Kazan, Mother of God of Smolensk, Three-Handed Mother of God! . . ."

Marya and Fekla crossed themselves and fasted, but knew nothing of religion. They neither taught their children to pray nor spoke to them of God; and they taught them no principles save that they must not eat meat during fasts. With the other villagers it was the same; few believed and few understood. Nevertheless, all loved the Scriptures, loved them dearly and piously; the misfortune was that there were no books and no one to read and explain, so that when Olga read aloud the Gospel she was treated with respect, and all addressed her and her daughter Sasha as " You."

At Church festivals Olga often walked to neigh-bouring villages, and even to the district town, where there were two monasteries and twenty-seven churches. She was abstracted, and as she walked on her pilgrimage forgot her family. When she returned home it seemed that she had only just discovered her husband and daughter, and she smiled and said radiantly—

"God has sent us His mercy!"

Everything that happened in the village repelled and tormented her. On Elijah's Day they drank, at Assumption they drank, at Elevation they drank. At Intercession Zhukovo had its parish festival; and this the muzhiks observed by drinking for three days; they drank fifty roubles from the communal funds; and then went round the huts and collected money for more vodka. On the first days the Tchikildeyeffs killed a ram, and ate mutton in the morning, at dinner, and for supper; and in the night all the children got out of bed to eat more. Kiriak was drunk all three days; he drank away his cap and boots, and beat Marya so badly that she had to be soused with water. And then all were sick with shame.

Despite this, even this Zhukovo, this Kholuefka, had once a real religious festival. That was in August, when through every village in the district was borne the Life-giving Ikon. The day it was due at Zhukovo was windless and dull. Early in the morning the village girls, in their bright, holiday dress, set out to

meet the ikon, which arrived at evening with a procession and singing; and at that moment the church
bells rang loudly. A vast crowd from Zhukovo and
neighbouring villages filled the street; there were
noise, dust, and crushing. And the old man, grandmother, and Kiriak—all stretched out their hands to
the ikon, looked at it greedily, and cried with tears—

"Intercessor, Mother! Intercessor!"

All at once, it seemed, realised that there is no
void between earth and heaven, that the great and
strong of this world have not seized upon everything,
that there is intercession against injury, against
slavish subjection, against heavy, intolerable need,
against the terrible vodka.

"Intercessor, Mother!" sobbed Marya. "Mother!"

When the service was said and the ikon carried away,
all things were as of old, and noisy, drunken voices
echoed from the inn.

Death was dreaded only by the wealthy muzhiks;
the richer they grew the less their faith in God and
in salvation; and only out of fear of the end of the
world, to make certain, so to speak, they lighted
candles in the church and said mass. The poorer
muzhiks knew no fear of death. They told the old
man and grandmother to their faces that they had
lived their day, that it was high time to die, and
the old man and grandmother listened indifferently.
They did not scruple to tell Fekla in Nikolai's presence

that when he, Nikolai, died, her husband, Denis, would get his discharge from the army and be sent home. And Marya not only had no fear of death, but was even sorry that it lingered; and she rejoiced when her own children died.

But though they knew no dread of death, they looked on sickness with exaggerated dread. The most trifling ailment, a disordered stomach, a slight chill, sent grandmother on to the stove, where she rolled herself up, and groaned loudly without cease, "I'm dying!" And the old man would send for the priest to confess her and administer the last sacrament. They talked eternally of colds, of worms, of tumours which begin in the stomach and slowly creep towards the heart. Most of all they dreaded colds, and even in summer dressed warmly, and cowered over the stove. Grandmother loved medical treatment, and constantly drove to hospital, where she said she was fifty-eight instead of seventy, for she feared that if the doctor knew her age, he would refuse to treat her, and would tell her it was time to die. She usually started for the hospital at early morning, taking a couple of the little girls, and returned at night, hungry and ill-tempered, with a mixture for herself and ointments for the girls. Once she took with her Nikolai, who for the next two weeks dosed himself with a mixture, and said that he felt better.

Grandmother knew every doctor, *feldscher*, and wise-

woman within thirty versts, and disapproved of all.
At Intercession, when the priest made his round of the
huts with a crucifix, the clerk told her that near the
town prison there was an old man, formerly an army
feldscher, who doctored cleverly, and he advised grandmother to see him.   She took the advice.   When the
first snow fell she drove into town, and brought back
an old, bearded Jew in a long caftan, whose whole face
was covered with blue veins.   At that time journey-
men worked in the hut : an old tailor in terrifying
spectacles made a waistcoat out of rags ; and two
young lads made felt for top-boots.   Kiriak, dismissed
for drunkenness, and now living at home, sat beside
the tailor and mended a horse-collar.   The hut was
close and smoky.   The Jew looked at Nikolai, and said
that he must be bled.

He applied leeches, and the old tailor, Kiriak,
and the little girls looked on, and imagined they
saw the disease coming out of Nikolai.   And Nikolai
also watched the leeches sucking his chest, and saw
them fill with dark blood ; and feeling that, indeed,
something was coming out of him, he smiled con-
tentedly.

"It's a good way!" said the tailor.   "God grant
that it does him good!"

The Jew applied twelve leeches to Nikolai, then
twelve more ; drank tea, and drove away.   Nikolai
began to tremble ; his face turned haggard, and—as

the women put it—dwindled into a fist; his fingers turned blue. He wrapped himself up in the counter-pane and then in a sheepskin coat; but felt colder and colder. Towards evening he was peevish; asked them to lay him on the floor, asked the tailor not to smoke, then lay still under the sheepskin; and towards morning died.

IX

It was a rough, a long winter.

Since Christmas there had been no grain, and flour was bought outside. Kiriak, who still lived at home, made scenes at night, causing terror to all; and next morning his head ached, and he was ashamed, so that it was painful to see him. Night and day in the stall a hungry cow lowed, and rent the hearts of grandmother and Marya. And to make things worse the frost grew severer, and the snow heaped itself high in the street, and the winter stretched out. Annunciation was marked by a genuine winter snow-storm, and snow fell in Holy Week.

But even this ended. The beginning of April brought warm days and frosty nights. Winter gave way reluctantly, but the hot sunshine foiled him, and at last the brooks melted and the birds began to sing. The fields and shrubs by the river-side were hidden in spring floods, and from Zhukovo to the village beyond stretched a big lake, given over to wild duck. The spring sunsets, fiery and with splendid clouds, yielded each day sights new and incredible, sights which are often laughed at when they appear on canvas.

The cranes cried mournfully, as if they called on men to follow them. Standing on the brink of the ravine, Olga looked at the flood, at the sun, at the bright, it seemed rejuvenated, church; and her tears flowed and she panted with passionate longing to go away, though it might be to the end of the earth. And indeed, it was decided that she should return to Moscow and seek a place as housemaid; and with her would go Kiriak to earn his living as dvornik, or somehow else. *Akh*, to get away soon!

When the roads dried and the weather turned hot they prepared for the journey. Olga and Sasha with wallets on their backs, both in bast-shoes, left at dawn; and Marya came to see them off. Kiriak, ill, remained for a week more. For the last time Olga prayed towards the church, and thought of her husband, and though she did not cry, her face wrinkled, and seemed ugly, as an old woman's. During the winter she had grown thinner, uglier, and a little grey; instead of the old charm and pleasant smile her face expressed submissiveness and sorrow outlived; and her look was dull and fixed as if she were deaf. She was sorry to leave the village

and the muzhiks. She remembered how they carried
away Nikolai; how mass was said at nearly every
hut; and how all wept, feeling her grief their own.
Summer and winter there were hours and days when
it seemed to her that these men lived worse than
beasts, and to look at them was terrible: they were
coarse, dishonest, dirty, drunken; they lived in dis-
cord; they fought eternally, because they despised,
feared, and suspected one another. Who kept the
drink shop and dosed the muzhik with drink? The
muzhik. Who squandered and spent on drink the
money of the commune, of the school, of the Church?
The muzhik. Who stole from his neighbour, burnt
his house, perjured himself in court for a bottle of
vodka? The muzhik. Who first spoke at the
Zemstvo and on other boards against the muzhik?
The muzhik. Yes; to live with them was torture!
But despite all this, they were men, they suffered
and wept as men; and in their whole lives there
was not one act for which an excuse might not be
found. Labour unbearable, from which the whole
body ached at night, fierce winters, scanty harvests,
crowding; help from nowhere, and no hope of help!
The richer and the stronger gave no help because
they themselves were rude, dishonest, intemperate,
and foul-tongued; the pettiest official or clerk treated
the muzhiks as vagabonds; even the cantonal chiefs
and Church elders addressed them as "Thou," and

believed they had a right thereto. Yes! And could there be help or good example from the selfish, the greedy, the dissolute, the idle, who came to these villages with but one intent: to insult, terrify, and rob? Olga remembered the piteous, humiliated faces of the old men when in winter Kiriak was brought out to be flogged! And now she was sorry for all these men and women; and on her last walk through the village she looked at every hut.

When she had accompanied them three versts Marya said good-bye; then fell upon her knees, and with her face touching the ground, cried loudly—

"Again I am left alone; alas, poor me, poor, poor, unfortunate! . . ."

And she continued to keen, so that long afterwards Olga and Sasha could see her on her knees, bent on one side, holding her head with her hands. And above her head flew rooks.

The sun rose higher: the day grew warm. Zhukovo was left far behind. The travellers followed many circuitous paths, and Olga and Sasha soon forgot the village and Marya. They were in good humour, and everything amused them. First a mound; then a line of telegraph posts, with mysterious humming wires, which vanished on the horizon, and sped to some unknown destination; then a farm, buried in green, which sent from afar a smell of dampness and hemp, and seemed to say that it was the home of happy people; then a horse's skeleton lying white in a field. And larks sang untiredly; quails cried to one another; and the landrail cried with a sound like the drawing of an old bolt.

At midday Olga and Sasha reached a big village, and, in the broad street, came upon General Zhukoff's old cook. He was hot, and his red, sweating bald patch shone in the sun. At first he did not recognise Olga; then he looked and recognised her, but both, without exchanging a word, continued their paths. Olga stopped and bowed low before the open windows of a hut which seemed richer and newer than its neighbours, and cried in a loud, thin, and singing voice—

" Orthodox Christians, give alms for the love of Christ; Kingdom of Heaven to your father and mother, eternal rest."

" Orthodox Christians," echoed little Sasha. "Give for the love of Christ, Heavenly Kingdom. . . . "